CW00499765

CANTE̶L̶N̶ ̶̶̶̶̶
THE NAAFI STORY

NATHAN MORLEY

Canteen Army

Copyright © 2018 by Nathan Morley

Cover image: RAF servicemen enjoy a cup of tea at an airbase in southern England during the summer of 1944. (Crown Copyright)

ISBN: 9781719947367 (Paperback edition)

ACKNOWLEDGMENTS

First and foremost, I would like to thank the many former Naafi employees that have taken the time to provide information and share their own personal memories and experiences.

The research part of this project, which turned out to be extremely enjoyable – and took me to Germany, the UK, Malta, and Crete – was made easier by the many helpful staff at the *British Library*, the PIO in Cyprus, *Kölnisches Stadtmuseum, National Archives* in London and the *Staatsbibliothek zu Berlin*.

I would also like to thank former British Defence Ministers Sir John Nott and Lord Michael Heseltine for their helpful contribution. Special thanks are extended to Kevin O'Kane, Doug Pullen, Kevin Royle, Eve Diett, Nicola Maksymuik, John Perry, Evan Morson-Glabik, Terry O'Reilly, Dieter Rudolph, Martin Bell OBE, Phil Shanahan, Phil Welsh, Ruth Mollett and, not least, my father Bernard Morley, who graciously took time to read through drafts of this manuscript, and being an ex-serviceman, provided sound advice and insights.

Contents

INTRODUCTION

Stamps or discount? Those words are familiar to anyone that has lived in the forces world and will forever be etched on my memory, as is the moment I saw a computer for the very first time – a chocolate brown *Commodore 64* – on display in the foyer of the JHQ Naafi in 1983. I remember standing in bewilderment with my parents, unsure what it actually did. We didn't buy one, thank God.

Later, as an adult working in Cyprus, Naafi reappeared in my life. Over the course of several years, I have delved deep into the history of this unique organisation and one thing I've discovered, is that it would be impossible to mention the countless heroic episodes in theatres of war and on the home front that helped to carve its reputation as a great British institution.

Firstly, those under the impression that Naafi was safely distanced from the fighting during their deployments are in for a surprise. It was never willing to be just a spectator and maintained the highest standards under shellfire, rocket attacks, air-raids and in the galleys of stricken Navy ships.

Secondly, Naafi worked alongside the remarkable men and women ensuring Britain's survival in the *Second World War*, and its continued security since then.

It is a sad fact that for anyone growing up during the latter half of the last century, the image of 'char and wad' provided the cut and dried impression of what the Naafi was – unfortunately, it's an extremely deceptive myth, which from time-to-time, continues to be peddled by the popular press.

But, as you will read, Naafi's value to Britain was far

more tangible than simply providing Forces with somewhere to relax and shop. Much of this book is devoted to the risks and challenges taken during the *Second World War* when every battle-weary infantryman appreciated Naafi the most. For air-crews, there was no finer moment than crashing out in a comfortable leather chair after making it home safely from a perilous bombing raid. Furthermore, whenever troops made a fresh landing, they found Naafi close on their heels, first opening bulk-issue stores in tents or ingeniously improvised cover, then, as the situation became more settled, acquiring, stocking and staffing large canteens offering food, entertainment, and other facilities. In some theatres, Naafi canteens were built from empty petrol cans and wrecked bomber fuselages; Far Eastern jungle fighters joked about those fashioned in palm leaves.

Even though it often gets a terrible ribbing, those who have served with the British Forces know what a remarkable job Naafi do in both war and peacetime. It is a very human organisation - the men and women of the institute, while sharing the dangers of their comrades in uniform, provide the small luxuries that make life in a war zone more bearable.

From serving dinners on the blood-soaked fields of Flanders to running shops in the recent brutal conflict in Afghanistan, Naafi remains a stupendous achievement.

Nathan Morley
Nicosia, September 4th, 2018

CHAPTER 1
ONWARD, CHRISTIAN SOLDIERS

UNTIL the middle of the 19th century, the sale of hard liquor to soldiers at regimental canteens was rampant and uncontrolled. Few officers raised an eyebrow at the sight of their men stumbling on to the parade ground with debilitating hangovers– these burley 'hard nuts' that could soak-up vast amounts of booze were known colloquially as 'sponges'.

This state of affairs wasn't surprising given that Victorian Britain was a society awash with alcohol, and although at times barracks could be filled with semi-paralytic soldiers, the government was reluctant to change such lunacy; especially as tax-revenues on liquor sold in army canteens reaped over £20,000 annually.

Early Victorian newspapers are filled with reports detailing the outrageous antics of drunken troops. At Limerick in Ireland, a resident demanded 'protection for society' after a group of inebriated soldiers 'assaulted respectable females' in the town centre. In Colchester, a quick browse of the local *Essex Standard,* reveals a similar picture. On one occasion, residents complained they were at the mercy of six drunken soldiers, who smashed in the windows of several houses on a warm May evening in 1856. 'They appeared to be mad drunk, and used their sticks for the purpose,' a witness wrote to the paper. 'Where did they obtain their drink? How did they get out of the camp? Where were the sentries? When are we next to be visited with a similar outrage? and where are we to seek protection from these gallant defenders of our country?' A month later, in the same town, another resident expressed fury that 'girls were in the habit of frequenting the *Military Road* at a late hour for the purpose of decoying drunken soldiers,' – unsurprisingly, venereal disease was rampant among many regiments.

Periodic boozy rampages, prostitution, and violence became the Bain of many law-abiding citizens in garrison towns across Britain.

The culprit, according to a former Irish Guard was the principal charges of army canteens, who were really 'publicans on a large scale.' It was only when Dr. William Fergusson piped-up about what he called 'institutions of drunkenness' that change came.

Fergusson, a former Inspector-General of Military Hospitals, said he found it difficult to believe how an 'abuse so monstrous' could have been tolerated for so long and to such an extent.[1] 'Spirits,' he concluded, 'were a nuisance to discipline, and harmful to the health of soldiers.' Doing his bit to correct this absurd situation, he let-rip with a campaign for change, which was backed by social reformers and succeeded in getting hard liquor banned from garrison canteens. The *Secretary of War* described the ban as 'one of the greatest blessings ever conferred upon the British army.'[2] But not everybody was happy. One 'most aristocratic' commander of a distinguished regiment complained that after the ban, crimes resulting from drunkenness had not decreased, and his medical officer had 'found no difference in the health of the men'. He was also furious that his troops began to resort to public houses in the neighbourhood 'where spirits are sold and the men are thus thrown more into the society of the civilians.'[3]

Such sentiments were echoed elsewhere. In the *Kerry*

---

[1] House of Commons debate 'Canteens in Barracks,' 5th March, 1847
[2] Baron Panmure, Minister of War. Maidstone Journal and Kentish Advertiser, 30th March, 1858.
[3] Cork Examiner, January 1st, 1849.

Evening Post, an article claimed the ban was 'not giving satisfaction' to military authorities as the consequence was 'more drunkenness and disease amongst the troops, owing to the deleterious compounds introduced into that liquor unprincipled traders outside barracks.'[4]

The new regulations stipulated that anyone wishing to operate army canteens had to 'clearly understand' that the sale of spirituous liquors was strictly prohibited and all applicants had to be of 'sober and generous spirit' and any person 'not of unexceptionable character' would be unsuitable.

Vacancies for contractors were frequently placed in newspapers by the *Board of Ordnance*,[5] with successful applicants paying rent, taxes, and commissions for the privilege of selling provisions to non-commissioned officers and privates. Where it was unprofitable for a contractor to set-up, there were no canteens. A quartermaster from the regiment was responsible to ensure that no irregularity occurred. With the ban in force, the seedy reputations of canteens began to gradually improve and the new regulations were generally respected and kept.

The canteens, though, remained grim places as profit-seeking businessmen continued to win concessions - and did well out of them. These businessmen were not protected against temptation. Sometimes the corruption was obvious – like tender manipulation and bribes to sell inferior brands, or using a certain supplier with the promise of kickbacks.

Excluding taxes and rent, their capital outlay was minimal – shelves for dry goods, wooden tables, a vaulted cellar for stock, benches and a bar for serving beer and

---

[4] Kerry Evening Post, November 18th, 1848
[5] Contracts were usually awarded to the highest bidders for one year.

wine. Nearly everything on sale was displayed in bulk and had to be weighed and wrapped. There was no pre-packed merchandise - huge casks of coffee, sugar, tea, and spices were dumped on the canteen floor. The shelves were stacked with jellies, jams, canned foods, pickles, and sauces.

Soldiers looking worst for wear at a barrack canteen, as depicted in the pages of the *Illustrated London News* in 1847.

One of the most appealing aspects of Victorian army life was the promise of regular meals, where for sixpence, soldiers were served breakfast at 7.30am and lunch at noon in the regimental mess. On a good day, cooks might dish-out blood sausage and boiled vegetables, with a dessert of sweet pie crust, or plum duff. An entire lexicon was born in the mess, where sausages were sometimes referred to as 'Bags o' Mystery' – 'because no man but the maker knows what is in them,' and at sea, a sailor confronted with 'bow wow mutton' thought meat was so bad 'it might be from a dog.' [6]

On the whole, it seems, the forces were agreeably reconciled to their lot, except when posted on missions abroad in harsh climates or disease-ridden areas, where mealtimes were approached with trepidation. Hardtack biscuits - dried to the point of mummification - and tinned 'bully' beef was often the only nourishment when fresh produce was not obtainable.

In these days before refrigeration, food preservation was crude and often dangerous. The lead-alloy solder used to seal tin cans was known to frequently seep into the contents causing nausea, vomiting, and diarrhoea. And there was nothing more horrifying than pouring the contents of a tin into a pan, only to discover it infested with maggots. Reports of the general public falling dangerously ill after consuming canned food were also common. Doctors frequently dealt with cases of vomiting, partial paralysis, and worse. Newspaper stories detailing how a mother and her son in Wolverhampton were poisoned by eating tinned salmon, or the pensioner in Leeds that died from the effects of eating canned lobster made the public weary.

Such provisions made life at sea equally appalling; with sailors often served inedible supplies to ward off starvation. In 1853, the crew of the *HMS Plover* threw 1,500lb of tinned meat overboard because they 'found it in a pulpy, decayed and putrid state, and totally unfit for men's food'.

Such conditions amplify the low regard the military was

---

[6] From: *Passing English of the Victorian Era* by Andrew Forrester.

held in at the time, as their welfare was overlooked with almost wilful ignorance by the government. Soldiers were considered by some as being the dregs of society, on par with navvies and other 'undesirables,' especially given that recruits were known to sign-up to escape a hand-to-mouth existence, whilst others accepted the Queen's shilling after being plied with drink by recruiting sergeants.

It was only with the steady expansion of the British Empire, that the lot of the soldier began to change, as their role became indispensable in securing the nation's prosperity. But it was the *Crimean War* in 1856 that really transformed attitudes, when the public learned army supplies often arrived late or were not distributed until they had gone bad - leading to the death of many men through disease.

There were also reports of the drunkenness prevailing among soldiers in the Crimea, - resulting in many crimes. The problem was blamed on local spirit vendors, and, above all, against rakee importers. Rakee, a local brew, was described by one correspondent as a, 'villainous spirit which inflames men's brains and sets them mad; it has all the abominable properties of fresh rum or new whisky, but it affects the nervous system more mischievously, and produces prostration, which frequently ends in death. It is dreadfully cheap, is colourless, like gin, with taste of bad anisette.'

When *Indian Rebellion* followed a year later, the exploits of British Army became a fixture in the popular press, where they received constant praise for their gallant endeavours.

The clergy also became sensitive to army welfare. The *Church Army*, which had been busy reclaiming hundreds of the 'worst characters' in civilian society, including 'drunkards, wife-beaters, and pugilists' stepped forward to help soldiers in need. Soon after, SAAFA – *The Soldiers' and Sailors' Families Association* – opened to provide care to military wives and families. The army itself also improved the way men were fed in messes, with the establishment of the 'Military Train' - the forerunner of the Army Service Corps – providing meat, bread and other essentials to regiments both in Britain and overseas.

It was forty-six years after Dr. William Fergusson won his ban on spirits in barrack canteens; that a group of officers decided other progressive reforms were needed to put an end to the bribery and corruption continuing to plague the canteen system, where stewards still had their palms greased to award tenders and supply contracts.[7] In 1894, they established the *Canteen and Mess Co-operative Society* as a mutual benefit society to buy supplies in bulk at the best price and sell them to canteens, whilst returning its profits to those that bought from it.

The society rented a warehouse in London's east-end, recording first-year takings of over £4,500. 'But,' according to Sir John William Fortescue, 'the advantages which it offered was quickly discovered by regiments, and, despite fierce competition from the firms that had enjoyed the monopoly of canteen business, its trade steadily increased.'

A debate about the new venture flared up on the letter pages of the *Army and Navy Gazette* where one reader asserted the society was a 'pure and simple middleman, and as such, quite unnecessary.' Whilst another correspondent 'praised the very fact that the greasing of the palm of the canteen steward became impossible when

---

[7] Military historian Lieut. Colonel Howard N. Cole noted that fortunes were made at the expense of the serviceman, with dishonest canteen stewards becoming 'a music hall joke.'

the society is dealt with is a very long step in the right direction.'[8]

Whilst cases of graft did decline, dodgy-deals survived elsewhere, as not every garrison chose to use the new society. One example was the much publicised 'Canteen Scandal' at the turn of the 20th century, which exposed army officers and civilians of unfairly awarding supply contracts to the Lipton's Company.

For a brief enlightened moment in 1906, the War Office proposed a new centralized body to run canteens – their idea, it seems, was to roll out the *Canteen and Mess Co-operative Society* (or a similar system) to every garrison in Britain and abroad. 'It is placed beyond dispute,' a War Office report stated, 'that the entrance of this Society into the canteen-trade considerably brought down the prices of the supplying firms, that ordinary competition had failed to obtain the best terms for the soldier.'

But the grand reforms plans were not to be, as the army argued central control would lead to 'more muddling and interference.' In turn, the War Office abandoned the plan and missed a vital opportunity to create a more coherent structure for the canteens. It would take eight more years - and an event of catastrophic proportions - before the issue was raised again.

Incidentally, it is interesting to note that the German armed forces had suffered many similar problems to those of their British counterparts – especially when it came to alcohol abuse.

German barrack canteens were first opened in 1890 in order to draw soldiers away from public-houses. By the turn of the century, the Prussian Army ordered:

---

[8] Army and Navy Gazette, 21st March, 1896.

The use of alcohol and alcoholic drinks during marches and exercises of all kinds, including those during manoeuvres, is prohibited. Alcoholic drinks, such as brandy, spirits of all sorts, alcoholic extracts, or beer in bottles, must not be carried or sold by sutlers to the men. The sale of brandy and spirituous liquors in canteens is forbidden to the men from 9 pm in the winter and from 10 pm in the summer. Such drinks must only be sold by the glass, not the bottle.

CHAPTER 2
THE FIRST WORLD WAR

THE WORLD was going mad, or that is how it seemed to German Admiral von Tirpitz, who wrote to his wife in October 1914 that, 'this war is really the greatest insanity in which white races have ever been engaged.'

The Admiral could have hardly imagined then that the conflict would spiral far beyond Europe and introduce the world to the horrors of chemical weapons, air-raids – as well as the toppling of a Tsar, a Kaiser, and an Emperor. Never before would so many men take up arms in a conflict which would leave nine million dead.

The war was a nationally-unifying event - everyone knew someone in uniform or working for the 'war effort'. Rallying to the call of Lord Kitchener, brothers, husbands, sons, lovers, and fathers enrolled from every home and class across the land. As troops marched to Victoria Station to catch 'Goodbye trains' - their wives stuffed chocolates and cigarettes from the platform kiosks into their men's rucksacks. Those that didn't have an ample supply of tobacco were in for a nasty surprise on arrival in France, as there were no canteens waiting to serve them such luxuries.

In hindsight, it seems scarcely conceivable that plans for a canteen did not exist, but as outlined in the last chapter, it was not for want of trying. To get out of this very tricky position, Whitehall asked the *Canteen and Mess Society* to run operations on the continent with the help of a few private contractors. In 1915 they merged to form the *Expeditionary Force Canteens* (EFC) - a unit providing 'small comforts and articles such, as they are used to purchasing in their canteens or regimental institutes.'[9]

The EFC was designated a War Office institution under the control of the Army Council, with some of its senior officials granted temporary commissions, while subordinates were all in uniform with varying ranks. The entire staff was recognized as being 'engaged in the performance of duties under Military Authority, and were, therefore, under Military Law.'

As troops poured onto the continent, it became apparent that the new unit was chronically under-equipped and beset by acute shortages of goods. In fact, on mobilization in March 1915 - a battered second-hand car was the only transport available to trundle along the front-lines delivering supplies to makeshift canteens.[10] Under the most trying conditions, depots and stores were knocked together in tents, barns, and huts in Boulogne, Calais, Dieppe, Havre and Rouen.

By spring, as half a million troops dug-in on the Western Front, the canteen service was struggling to cope.[11] Whilst the lack of sufficient supplies and service could be irritating, as a rule - EFC always tried to serve the man in the fighting line first and the Tommy in the rear zone second, as for those at the front existing in muddy trenches, the little comforts were vital for morale.

---

[9] On Friday 5th March 1915, the War Office stated that the *Canteen and Mess Co-operative Society*, along with Dickeson's Ltd, had formed the *Expeditionary Force Canteen Co-operative Society*. Neither firm took any share of the profits, the whole of which was 'devoted to the good of the soldier and his dependents.'

[10] At this point the 'Front' stretched from the Belgian seafront to the Swiss border.

[11] By late 1915, 200 canteens were placed various points as close as possible to the trenches and billets, and these in turn supplied the Regimental Canteens with what they needed in the way of creature comforts.

'Mud is a bad description: the soil was more like a thick slime,' journalist Henry Williamson, who served in the trenches, noted. 'When walking one sank several inches in and, owing to the suction, it was difficult to withdraw the feet.'

The trenches were filthy; many were riddled with disease, flies, lice, rats and in some cases, rotting corpses. Dire sanitation and lack of proper medical care compounded matters - typhus, bronchitis, diarrhoea, dysentery, and flu was common. Almost all soldiers suffered from constipation, given the vast amount of tinned foods which were sent out in ration packs.

In November 1915, EFC Private William Noakes was running a canteen on the southern point of the British lines at Albert on the River Somme, where he experienced cooking 'amid the din of battle and to the accompaniment the roar of the big guns from batteries.' He was exposed to the full fury of enemy guns, as all hands were on fixed duty from 6 am to 9 pm serving troops coming and going to and from the trenches at all hours.[12]

Strikingly, even in such hellish conditions, some regiments successfully set up their own private canteens. The entrepreneurial men of the *6th Black Watch* converted a reserve dug-out into a cafe, which became a great 'draw' with three thousand eggs being sold in its first week. 'They were a treat, and the cooks have been kept busy boiling and frying them,' a member of the regiment remembered. The Rev. G. H. Donald from Aberdeen, serving as a chaplain with the Gordon Highlanders, was also convinced opening a canteen in his trench would lift spirits.

---

[12] Middlesex Chronicle, November 6th, 1915.

Trench life soon begins to tell on the mind and spirits. Besides the constant menace of the enemy through rifle fire and bombs and shells, there the oppressiveness of being shut up in a narrow valley without the pleasures and amenities accorded to Rasselas.[13] There is no outlook or chance of change, only the monotony of endless trenches and the damp, cold touch of earth and stone.

With the Gordon Highlanders trenches far out of reach of amenities, Donald set up his own small-scale effort buying food at an EFC store eight miles behind the line and conveying them by wagon to the mouth of a communication trench.

There, a party of stalwart Gordon's shouldered the lot, and in dark, dismal night rain and mud, carried the stuff up the reserve trench. It was an easy matter next morning to open the boxes and set them in a hurriedly erected shelter and begin sales. The men crowded round the place, and in a few hours, the lot had gone. The boys had sardines and tinned pears at dinner that day, and most men sported a packet of Woodbines.[14]

Such endeavours, whilst welcomed, were prohibited from buying their stock from sources other than the *Expeditionary Force Canteens*, which allowed a five percent discount on wholesale orders. Securing produce from local shops and farms was frowned upon, and the same

---

[13] The Prince of Abyssinia: A tale, though often abbreviated to Rasselas, is an apologue about happiness by Samuel Johnson.
[14] Aberdeen Evening Express, April 3rd, 1916.

purchasing rules applied to the considerable voluntary movement emerging to serve the troops pouring into France, with small shops, cafes, and libraries.

Along with the *YMCA, Catholic Women's League* and *Church Army*, independent efforts like 'Miss Barbour's canteen' sprang up in the coastal town of Etaples.[15] Her influence can be seen in the pages of the *Globe* newspaper, which reported: 'Miss Barbour has given of her means to make the fighting men happy. There is a convalescent camp at Etaples, and they all patronize her excellent canteen. Miss Barbour is the cheeriest manageresses. No praise can be too high for the work she is doing.'[16] Further north in Boulogne, socialite Lady Angela Forbes unfolded a trestle table every night on the railway station platform to serve soldiers with tea and cake.

Another extraordinary effort, which has been largely overlooked, was known as the *Women's Emergency Canteens*, founded by a Mrs. Wilkie in 1915 for the express purpose of providing refreshment and recreation rooms free for French soldiers in France. Her offer of help was accepted by the French military authorities, under whose direction the work was carried out. British ladies that went out to France with the canteens got nearer to the actual firing line than any other women, except nurses. The work of those brave women remained little known or appreciated in England.

---

[15] This was the scene of huge concentrations of Commonwealth reinforcement camps and hospitals.

[16] *Voluntary effort and the canteens* by a special correspondent. *The Globe*, Tuesday 10th August, 1915. The article adds: 'Don't let it be thought that the EFC's are not doing all they can. Their canteens are run on excellent business lines.'

Away from the voluntary efforts and the refined atmosphere of Lady Forbes tea urn, EFC staff near the front lines– all officially non-combatants – frequently stiffened the ranks by acting as stretcher bearers and on occasion even picking up arms to join the fight. Canteens often doubled up as make-shift medical tents, whilst at the larger field hospitals, tea trolleys clattered along the wards serving refreshments, as travelling kitchens churned out hot meals on troop-trains.

The canteens provided a welcome break from the horrors of the front line. Here, troops in France enjoy a beer and dinner at a canteen under canvas, circa 1917.

As the war rumbled on, EFC continued to grow; becoming the universal provider with 577 branches in France and in Flanders. An original well-thumbed stock list from 1916 shows they were selling a dizzying array of products ranging from ammonia and anchovies to dictionaries and curry powder. Their solitary automobile had been replaced by 249 trucks, 151 cars, and 42 motorcycles.

From EFC headquarters at the chateau Regnière–Eclusenear on the Somme, managers oversaw hundreds of mobile kitchens, butcheries, bakeries, cinemas, concert parties, printing presses, and a ration pack production depot. There was a mineral water factory, established by fluke when Captain E.C. White, the overseas manager, stumbled upon a derelict spring run by a French company on its last legs. From there he began producing soda-water and selling it at three francs for a dozen bottles. White also started making ginger beer which sold like hot cakes.

Over time, the canteens gained a reputation for being careful about credit, with troops affectionately referring to the EFC as 'Every Franc Counts' because of their shrewd business practices – and flat refusal to accept IOUs. There were no sales of over-the-counter alcohol either, and spirits were supplied only to officers and sergeants' messes and were only obtainable with signed authority from a staff officer - meaning it was never possible for a private soldier to obtain spirits.[17] EFC did brew beer on the continent as well as gathering wine directly from vineyards in France, Italy, Spain and Portugal.

But at the shops, the big sellers were always cigarettes and chocolate. A soldier from the *65th Divisional Cyclist Company* described how he had never seen anything 'quite so awful' as the EFC during the Christmas of 1917; it 'was worse,' he said, 'than a bargain sale. There were no

---

[17] During the last year of the war, EFC attempted to calculate the average weekly consumption of whisky by officers on all the fighting fronts. A very general assumption concluded that 25 per cent of the total number officers drank no whisky at all, and on that basis, the amount consumed per head per week for the remainder worked out at three-quarters of bottle.

ladies, of course, but the queue of officers was worse than any queue of feminine remnant-hunters-if possible. After a hand to hand, catch-as-catch-can skirmish lasting an hour and a quarter, I gained a few inches of the counter.'[18]

Contrary to popular belief, troops did not spend all of their time in the trenches or preparing for battle – they were rotated between the front lines, reserve trenches and spent leisure time in rear areas where bigger canteens, shop huts, and rest-houses were staffed by members of the *Woman's Army Auxiliary Corps* (WAAC), working for the EFC. The WAAC volunteers, donned in their 'khaki' uniforms and small rounded-cap, became a welcome sight for Allied forces everywhere.

A leave club on the Western Front, either 1917 or 1918.

In an attempt to stretch limited supplies, the girls used

---

[18] Letter to the *Cyclometere*.

inventive methods such as dipping rashers of bacon into flour to 'beef them up,' or soaking stale bread in water and then baking it again. Their dedication in the midst of havoc and desolation was singled out for special mention by Captain Viedenburg of the *10th London Regiment*.

> They (the WAAC) have behaved most admirably under, at times, very trying circumstances. They have been through raid after raid at Boulogne, Abbeville, and Etaples. At Abbeville their camp was totally demolished before their eyes by bombs, while they took shelter in trenches. Another time, their hostel and all their possessions were destroyed whilst they encamped in the neighbouring woods; after that, the women were moved to another camp. This was also wrecked in front of them, and twenty minutes later, while all were congratulating themselves once; more a lucky escape, a small bomb fell right in the trench, killing eight.[19]

Viedenburg described how in Boulogne it was frequently necessary to scarper to the dug-outs the middle of dinner, and as soon the all-clear signal sounded the women returned their work serving at the mess. Combined with occasional leave to England, the system of huts and rest-houses managed to keep most men sane. Soldiers could idle away hours in a club, with the good meal and fully stocked bar:

> Everything that could be thought of to make men forget the horrors of the front was to be found at

---

[19] Viedenburg authored an independent observer's account of the workings of the EFC after the war.

these clubs and rest-houses; not merely good fare—though there is no more comforting change to a war-worn man than change of diet—but neatness, cleanliness, comeliness and attention, in fact all that could most agreeably contrast with emergency-rations and the sound and smell of slaughter.[20]

***

Obtaining little luxuries at postings further afield; like in Salonika, proved trickier as the battle to keep supplied kept shelves Spartan. Rifleman William Walls expressed dismay after 'having to stand in a line for about two hours before getting served. Then I only got a small packet of tea and some cigarettes for my pal.'[21] Walls - like most of his comrades - was not satisfied. Pricey items topped his list of grumbles: 'I went to the British *Expeditionary Force Canteen* and spent ten drachmas on milk, fruit, and a tin of salmon. We received our pay in the afternoon I got fifteen drachmas.'

Over in Gallipoli, where the allies were failing to score a victory against the Ottoman Empire, Sergeant Harrop of the *Divisional Engineers* was also miffed. Even though the army maintained discipline and fighting spirit in the midst of disaster, Harrop's published grumbles were not far off the mark of truth. No doubt soldiers would be frantic to buy goods if there was anybody selling them, 'but the troops in France have the *Expeditionary Force Canteens*

---

[20] John Fortescue noted the rest houses provided bed, baths, library, a quiet space to catch up on reading and writing, a games room and a full-time barber in his book *A Short Account of Canteens in the British Army*. The University Press, 1928.

[21] Wills served with the 4th Battalion, Kings Royal Rifles.

trotting about all over the show and can fairly easily get almost anything they want,' he noted bitterly. 'The troops out here have no facilities for purchasing little odd things which would probably add to their comfort.'[22] His experience was unfortunate, as the EFC did eventually operate in the Dardanelles (four months after the first troops arrived) and during the evacuation of Gallipoli, but the problems shipping stock from Britain meant buying vast quantities of produce from Egypt and the Aegean Islands.

When thousands of barrels of Scottish beer did get through by sea, the army was convinced it was responsible for stopping the spread of dysentery, which was rife among the troops.

Those posted in Mesopotamia (modern day Iraq) enjoyed a more relaxed pace of life, fussed over by EFC waiters - garbed in white jackets – as they sipped afternoon teas at Qurna, the legendary site of the *Garden of Eden*. But, the drawbacks of such an exotic posting included the intense heat, which made ice and mineral waters a necessity, rather than a luxury.

> The base here was at Basra and since the principal means of communication was by water, the EFC soon set up a floating canteen on a stern-wheel steamboat. There were at one time thirty-seven in Mesopotamia, going up and down the Euphrates from Basra to Baghdad, beyond which they spread out fanwise to north and south and even into Persia.[23]

---

[22] Corporal's Racy Description of Trenches: 'Life in Gallipoli to be untenable.' Daily Gazette for Middlesbrough, 31st July, 1915.

[23] *A Short Account of Canteens in the British Army* by Sir John William Fortescue. The University Press, 1928

Over in Palestine and Egypt the canteens pushed forward their comforts on mules and camels to a line of outlets spread along the Suez Canal, where about £5million passed over counters annually.

Back in Europe, fatigue and exasperation had set in when Germany launched a massive offensive in March 1918, which became the biggest breakthrough on the Western Front, dashing hopes that the war was coming to an end. As thousands of artillery shells and missiles shot through the air, canteen workers carried on everywhere until evacuation orders were issued. Any stock which couldn't be moved was destroyed along with anything that might be useful to the enemy.[24]

Back in Britain, the population was also feeling the burden of war as a food crisis caused by submarine attacks on merchant vessels resulted in dwindling supplies and higher prices. To make matters worse, poor harvests meant that even staples like potatoes were becoming scarce.

On barracks across Britain – an official *Army Canteen Committee* had been formed in 1916 to service the 1,800 home canteens. Warehousing, staffing, and supply were whittled down a single central authority – spelling the end for the 150 private contractors that had still been making a lucrative living from home bases. 'The contractor has had his day,' Lord Cheylesmore, its first chairman declared, 'the army now wished, and quite rightly, to run its own business and to save money, and to improve the conditions of its canteens.'

With the food shortages, a priority was to increase local produce for the army, without making inroads upon

---

[24] EFC personnel suffered numerous casualties and several Meritorious Service Medals were awarded for fearless devotion to duty.

civilian requirements. With that in mind, the *Army Canteen Committee* encouraged smallholders and large producers to farm uncultivated land and increase acreage.[25] But, even such efforts could not stave off rationing.[26] Government minister Austen Chamberlain went further by pushing for the rations home-based troops to be slashed, arguing that the Army Service Corps and Army canteen rations together gave each man 3,800 calories, whilst the ordinary civilian received just 2,700 calories. Chamberlain argued:

> It is represented to us that the 600,000 men in the home army can on the merits of their Army Service Corps rations alone spare 2 *ounces* of meat a day, and that if they are to continue to receive Navy and Army Canteen Board supplies on their present scale, including 1 1/7th *ounces* of offal, they ought to spare a further 2 *ounces* of meat a day. We recommend that the War Office be offered the alternative of keeping variety and a reasonably large ration by parting with 4 *ounces* of meat a day from 600,000 men, or of suffering a drastic restriction of their Navy and Amy Canteen Board supplies. If we could save 2,400,000 *ounces* of meat a day, this is roughly equivalent to a gift of 2,000 tons a month, and it sets free a valuable addition of rations for the hard manual labourer.[27]

In a terse response, the War Office warned Chamberlain

---

[25] Over 10,000.000 barrels of beer was brewed in their first year of operation, whilst in Scotland, potato growers delivered 10 per cent of their crop for army use.

[26] Rationing was introduced in early 1918.

[27] War Cabinet document GT3990, marked 'Secret': "Rations of the home army and supplies for the Navy Canteen Board". Memorandum by Austin Chamberlain, March 21st, 1918.

to remember that 'the soldier is compelled by law to serve, and the corollary of this obligation is equitable treatment by his employer - the State.' The Army argued that the state had no more right to take advantage of the soldier's position than a parent has to take advantage of the 'helpless position' of a child.

**

The prayers of those hoping for an end to the conflict were answered in late 1918 when the Austro-Hungarian Empire and Germany agreed to an armistice ending the war in victory for the Allies in November.

By that point, the *Army Canteen Committee* had been remodeled as the *Navy and Army Canteen Board* (NACB), which in-turn incorporated the *Expeditionary Force Canteens* along with its operations in overseas theatres.[28] This amalgamation was not without controversy, as a spat about sharing wartime profits erupted. As hundreds of canteens wound down operations in Britain and abroad, some argued their profits should be divided among forces charities, whilst others claimed the canteens were being liquidated at a loss and there was no dividend to share.

Eventually, a *United Services Fund*, incorporated by Royal Charter, was formed to disburse the so-called 'canteen millions' under the chairmanship of Lord Byng. 'The story had become almost as intricate as a maze,' the *Pall Mall Gazette* observed. [29] The fund did dish-out money to worthy causes, but the situation was never decisively

---

[28] As well as the *Canteen and Mess Society*, *Dickeson's* and all other forces contractors.

[29] Byng said: 'No sticky fingered individual will ever touch one pound of the £7 million which we are distributing among the serving and ex serving soldiers'.

resolved and many ex-servicemen and their families cried foul. The scandal would remain a constant blot on the reputation of the canteen service.

**

As operations wound down, prodigious quantities of canteen material were thrown upon the market—everything from cookers to chocolate biscuits was sold off.

This sudden glut of merchandise turned out to be a blessing for Jack Cohen, an enterprising young former soldier who spent his £30 demob money on a crate-load of old EFC stock. He then hired a wheel-barrow and pitched up a stall to flog his consignment of *Lyle's Golden Syrup*, *Maconochie's Paste* and tins of Nestlé's canned milk (labeled for French troops).[30] He made a £1 profit on his first-day trading and returned the following morning to the EFC to buy more surplus stock. This enterprise would blossom into the supermarket giant Tesco.

Cohen later said he was convinced that 'almost anybody who is willing to pile it high, sell it cheap and work as I did, from five in the morning until midnight and even later, can make a fortune.'

Even with much of its wartime stock gone and the majority of canteens wound-up, there was still a military and they continued to need a canteen service.

So, in 1920, War Secretary Winston Churchill looked at the establishment of an institute to serve all armed forces at home and abroad during peacetime. The upshot was the dissolution of the *Navy and Army Canteen Board* and the birth of the *Navy, Army and Air Force Institutes* – or

---

[30] The Making of Tesco: A Story of British Shopping by Sarah Ryle, Bantam Press, 2013.

Naafi.

Just like the *Canteen and Mess Co-operative Society,* the new Naafi charter stated that all profits must be returned to the members of the forces in three ways: by the provision of entertainments and amenities, by cash payments into ships' and regimental funds, and by discounts to individual customers of Naafi shops. A council would decide on matters of policy and consist of twelve officers, four from each service, while a board would manage the commercial affairs through a general manager and comprise of three service representatives and three civilians experienced in commerce.

Jack Cohen

Other points worth mentioning are that canteen premises were to be provided by the Admiralty, War Office, and Air Ministry, and it was the task of Naafi to find necessary stock, furnishings, and staff and to make the best of the accommodation provided.

Naafi was also obliged to establish a branch wherever a Commanding Officer showed that 'the strength of his personnel exceeds the minimum for which a canteen service must be provided as required by War Office regulations.' Naafi had no choice in the matter - however remote and uneconomic the site or whether such an establishment ran at a profit or loss.

CHAPTER 3
COLOGNE

WITH Germany defeated, British troops marched into the Rhineland in December 1918 to begin an occupation that would last a decade.[31]

Their new home in Cologne morphed into an extension of the British Empire, as 12,000 soldiers - many with family in tow – decamped for an untroubled existence as though they were in Aldershot or India.[32] Cologne, with its assembly of middle-aged towers, spires, and ancient market squares, was one of the great treasures of Europe.

On arrival, the military government set up comfortably at the *Excelsior Hotel* just opposite the Gothic cathedral. In the hotel attic, two *Expeditionary Forces Canteen* officers managed to cobble together a staff of 120 men and women and set out on an expansion far beyond serving beer and tea.[33]

During the harsh winter of 1918-1919, when snow-blizzards and then widespread flooding caused havoc, EFC opened 'upmarket food hall' exclusively for officers and their wives, selling everything from shoes to house-cured sausages. With considerable ingenuity, a wood-

---

[31] The Allied occupation of the Rhineland took place following the armistice that brought the fighting of World War I to a close on November 11th, 1918. The occupying armies consisted of American, Belgian, British and French forces.

[32] They published a newspaper, ran clubs and even a theatre for amateur plays, where, according to the *St. Louis Star and Times* 'pretentious productions' ranged in style from melodrama to farce.

[33] EFC operated until 1st July, when the *Navy and Army Canteen Board* took over, and latterly Naafi.

panelled refreshment room with emerald upholstery and cane seating was opened next-door, serving 'British ladies and gentlemen fancy cakes and pastries.'

Naafi tried to keep up with new and ever-changing trends. The bigger retailers in Britain were getting creative, and - according to the *Leeds Mercury* - provided a 'satisfying spaciousness, a cheeriness of outlook, and careful planning of departments designed to enable customers to make their purchases with the minimum of fatigue.'

Even before the war, retailers were promoting the idea that shopping could be pleasurable. For example, the *Matthias Robinson* department store in Leeds became something of a showpiece with its arcade, large window display, showrooms on the first, second, third floors and central heating throughout. A notable feature was the basement, which had been converted into 'a well-lighted and ventilated floor' for the sale of goods, linens, and blankets. The first floor was entirely devoted to drapery, such as dress materials, gloves, silks, art needlework, lace goods, and blouses. The second floor comprised of several departments, including mantles, costumes, furs, millinery, ladies' and children's outfitting, and underclothing. On the third floor, the departments were for carpets, linoleums, bedding, bedsteads, and general furnishing goods.

A beautifully-furnished cafe, where lunch could be obtained and afternoon tea was served, looked out on Briggate and Kirkgate, as a capable orchestra performed hits of the day. Another innovation was shopping by post, which ladies apparently found 'much less irksome' than doing it in person.

Back in Germany, the *Cologne Post* noted that there were many minor ventures and improvements being inaugurated by the canteen services:

> … which will tend to brighten the existence of such of us as are forced to sojourn in this strange land. We briefly outline some of them. Saturday evening family dances are being held at the Marricer Hotel, where everyone knows everyone else, and a very comfortable and enjoyable evening may be spent by lovers of dancing and sociability. An invitation from a resident is all that is necessary to gain admittance.[34]

Lower down the pecking-order, enlisted men became loyal regulars at a canteen in the old town, which one soldier described as 'a real boon to Tommy and Jack.'[35] Expressing his joy to the *Cologne Post* newspaper, the same soldier declared that the canteen formed 'a perfect oasis in the desert of military life…without this institute our soldiers and sailors would pass a very dreary and monotonous time on the Rhine.'

Moselle wines and local beers became popular tipples, with many men enjoying their very first taste of wine and schnapps. Frothy pints of British-style beer began flowing at a club established at the ancient *Stapelhaus* in a grimy street, where the rain always formed huge puddles along the pavement. There, the pungent fragrance of steak pies and fish and chips wafted skywards into the *Museum of Natural History* which was located on the second floor. The constant smell of frying-fat became the Bain of the museums' curators. For the British though, it was a

---

[34] Cologne Post, October 15th, 1919
[35] This canteen was on Sternengasse.

perfect situation, as one reporter recounted: 'when the boys have enjoyed some rest and refreshment, they can proceed to contemplate a really wonderful collection of stuffed animals above.' Another British correspondent was even more enthusiastic:

> The Club is served by an efficient staff of girls whose uniform is a now a familiar sight in the streets of Cologne. When engaged in their duties they wear a most becoming blue overall. A peep into the kitchen is a revelation of how well things are done. Here many dainty dishes are prepared. The whole club is a busy hive of industry and is spotlessly clean. All the arrangements for the comfort and happiness of the men are well planned and carefully carried out.[36]

Opening shops and canteens were only the first hurdles to overcome, as troop's required constant entertainment and distractions. So, for a special treat, EFC requisitioned two paddle boats for pleasure trips along the Rhine.[37] Dorothy E. McKechine remembered everything was done for the comfort and welfare of the Tommy during her experience.[38] 'In the afternoons there are football and hockey matches, after which the home team gives tea to both parties which, of course, is prepared and served by our staff, and it is usually something nice and warm and savory which they enjoy after their strenuous playing.'

EFC also opened their own 'workers club' where whist drives and dances were held weekly. Entertainment was

---

[36] The *Cologne Post* September, 1919

[37] An idea revived two decades later in war-wrecked Berlin on the Wannsee and Havel.

[38] She joined the institute in 1924 serving in Cologne.

usually concluded by 11pm with the collective singing of 'God Save the King'.

EFC ladies organised their own sporting events and even the occasional theatrical production.

Wednesdays became a red-letter day, as the weekly wagonloads of supplies from Blighty chuntered into the Hauptbahnof railway station. 'No one ever sees a canteen without a queue in front of it and on Wednesdays it grows to almost immoderate proportions,' a correspondent observed.

At EFC stores, *Empire Shopping Week* – which emphasised the 'superiority of British goods' - became an annual fixture designed 'to inspire sense of pride in being associated with such a group of nations as those which owe allegiance to the Union Jack.'[39]

Employees were encouraged to go 'all out' in arranging attractive displays as a 'tribute to the past exploits of those who served.'

Whilst customers were advised to 'think British before buying foreign... as we arrange these displays let us remember that we must not be altogether sentimental …there is often a lot of British money behind many goods which are foreign'. It was noted that: 'British goods, and citizens would display not only patriotism but sound commercial sense if they insisted, for the specified period least, in demanding only Empire made goods. The experience would be such that the habit of British buying - would be not a matter of a week's duration, but a permanent feature of the housewife's shopping.'

---

[39] The in-house publication,(known as organ) of the NACB.

Customers were encouraged to 'Buy British,' with employees told to go 'all out' in arranging attractive displays as a 'tribute to the past exploits of those who served.'

The Germans, meanwhile, were minding their own business. 'Life in Cologne is very pleasant for the occupying army,' remarked Violet Markham, but regarding the local population, 'the post-war chaos appears so complete that men turn from it in despair.'[40] Away from the cocoon of the British community, the mayhem of a growing food shortage and hyperinflation was sweeping across Germany.

With hundreds of Germans working at British canteens – most of them unable to make ends meet - pilfering became rife. The authorities came down hard on the crimes they discovered. Those caught often faced draconian punishments, and even minor offences

---

[40] In her book *A Woman's Watch on the Rhine.*

frequently led to prison. Karl Franz, a 23-year-old waiter, was handed an unduly harsh six-month sentence for stealing ten forks, six knives, spoons, and a teapot, whilst in another case, a cook was sent to prison for six-weeks for taking 30-marks from the petty cash box.

At a British Summary Court, charwoman Anna Litzba was charged with stealing three billiard balls, two tablecloths, and eighty cigarettes and was sent to jail, whilst Katherine Esbach, a kitchen worker at the Naafi *Corner House* café, was jailed for a day for stealing half a pound of tea.

In the case of Maria Schmitz, a widow charged with being in possession of various articles of army clothing and a quantity of canteen stores, the presiding officer moaned about the 'dishonesty of civilians' employed by the British, lamenting that 'we trust these German civilians by employing them...but invariably they take advantage and rob us. I have not the slightest doubt that there is a systematic robbery of the British Government.'[41]

---

[41] The British Military courts, along with the occupation forces – and Naafi - eventually left Cologne in January 1926, but some troops remained stationed in nearby Wiesbaden until June 1930.

CHAPTER 4
PEACEFUL

SIXTEEN-YEAR-OLD Harry Banham was filled with wanderlust when he joined Naafi in 1921, but being so young; his dreams of camping in tropical climates had to wait. Unperturbed, he settled for a job as a store-man in London, where he witnessed the opening of the new Naafi headquarters at *Imperial Court*.

The four-storey Georgian structure on Kennington Lane was set apart by iron railings and built around a private courtyard under the shadow of the Oval gasometer. It was no typical workplace. When the foundation stone was laid; author Charles Dickens – then a jobbing newspaper reporter - was on hand to document the moment and local MP Charles Tennyson d'Eyncourt (uncle of the poet Alfred Lord Tennyson) presided over a special dinner to mark the occasion in 1836.

Nowadays, luxury apartments occupy the building and the nearby ramshackle warehouses have long since gone, but its past still resonates. 'At any hour of the day may come a cable from the furthest ends of the earth ordering goods for immediate dispatch,' observed the Rev. E. L. Macassey, writing about his visit to *Imperial Court* in 1926. Macassey described his astonishment at seeing the Naafi fleet of 100 vans stationed around the corner. 'The tinkle of a bell, a brisk answer, and the mighty wheels of this complicated mechanism revolve to meet the needs of some sun-baked Institute in the tropics.'

The old Naafi headquarters at Imperial Court in 2018 (Photo: Nathan Morley)

He watched the staff that oversaw hundreds of general stores, mobile kitchens, beer canteens, billiard saloons, and tearooms, as accountants poured over eye-wateringly large takings. The first thing that stuck teenager E.G. Goater, who joined Naafi as a messenger boy in 1928, was the sheer scale of the endeavor. 'Ting! Ting! Ting! echoed in my ears from the time clocks as the various members of the staff: men, boys, women, and girls clocked in. One after another they came to work in an endless stream, just like a queue filling into a theatre.'

Goater spent most his time darting between *Imperial Court* and Naafi warehouses in White Hart Street. 'When I first saw the bakery, I was amazed,' he recalled. In fact, the sweet aroma of fresh bread and cakes would waft through the nearby streets, much to the delight of local residents. Slapstick comedian Charlie Drake often told the story of how he worked as a baker in Kennington, gaining notoriety for his fruitcakes, until he was dismissed for using too many rationed currants.

Goater also remembered the bacon stoves, furniture warehouse, hardware stores, groceries provisions department and staff shop. 'I was also impressed with the huge Printing Department, where stationary used in the business, Christmas cards and other things for the services were printed.' Most workers at *Imperial Court* became familiar with the colourful slang which had developed at Naafi canteens, where a 'wad' meant a scone and 'fly cemetery' was an acidic reference to a Naafi sandwich.

One of the first practical exercises new recruits had to learn about was currency exchange. Coming to grips with that took place in classrooms on the upper floors, where they were taught to trade with the Palestine pound, Egyptian piastres, and Iraqi dinars.

Those posted to Cairo had to understand that there were 100 piastres to the pound, but in neighbouring Syria, there were just 900. In Abyssinia 'Maria Theresa' dollars were used, while in Kenya, shillings and Indian rupees became mixed. In later years, the problem of the Greek drachma was added, which, as one official put it 'always end in a recurring decimal.' Accounting was made a little easier by the installation of fifteen 'fanfold billing machines' which could process five million items annually.

Between 1923 and 1926, Naafi embarked on a huge refurnishing scheme at all institutes, both in Britain and abroad. This was the period when the 'Naafi style' emerged, which would eventually be adopted by all institutes. During the works, Naafi purchased:

11,500 tables 1,580 mirrors, 31,000 small chairs, 1,300 menu frames. 16,000 arm chairs, 1,180 show-stands, 3,400 easy chairs, 14,100 electric light shades, 670 settees and wall seats, 7,700 mats of various types, 700 Billiard seats, 30 acres of floor covering, 7,700 pictures, 59 miles of material for curtains, 1,300 clocks and 1,600 notice boards.

On completion of the project, *Imperial Club Magazine* noted:

Since the completion of the scheme the quantities of Easy Chairs, Settee and Wall Seats have been very greatly increased. It is not, of course, to be expected that such a huge task as this could be undertaken and completed without a fair amount of criticism arising, but on this score all that need be said is that some of the criticisms were constructive. Even the important question of the colours of lino and curtains was overcome, although many humorous incidents arose there from. For instance, a Commanding Officer would decide that a certain colour was the only possible shade to adopt for his Institute. At a later date, his predecessor considered it was the possible colour and the Naafi must have been mad when they supplied it.

With their sophisticated communication network, Naafi was able to keep in constant contact with its entire empire via telegraph, phone and, shortwave radio. Daily telegrams were blinked out to Portsmouth, the home of the Royal Navy, where a small motor launch served harbour vessels and repair crews working on laid up ships. Beneath her raised hatch, sat neatly stowed food in packets and tins—necessities, luxuries, fresh fish and vegetables, tobacco, toothpaste, sauces and condiments, sewing utensils, sweets, and medicines.

A NCS bookstall onboard *HMS Renown*, 1923.

In the bitter winter of 1932, Naafi was called upon to give 'hands-on' help to navy salvage crews recovering a stricken submarine.

The M2 tragedy became the focus of huge media attention after she vanished during manoeuvres with 60 men onboard. The submarine was used as an experimental aircraft carrier and sank after a hangar door was left open; she was found 18 fathoms deep in *Dead Man's Bay*, off Portland Bill, with all hands lost. From the very start of the epic recovery effort, at the request of the captain of the main salvage vessel the *HMS Adamant*, Naafi kept a motor launch on the scene, with her crew not only serving tea, but helping in the actual salvage operation – by installing pumping and winching equipment onto their canteen boat. Divers were handicapped by the fact that the M2 was lying in a maze of fierce currents known as Portland Race. The *Derby Daily Telegraph* reported her bow was deep in the sand and her stern stood several feet above the seabed:

> One or two divers who went down this afternoon were brought to the surface in a semi-conscious condition. As soon as divers go down they are swept by the tides until they lie parallel with the sea bottom, and it is only at low tide that they stand a reasonable chance of actually reaching the wreck.

Four pontoons, like huge steel drums, were deployed to buoy up the sunken vessel. Two were chained to the stern and two to the bow.

TheM2 had her big gun removed. In its place was fitted a water-tight hangar in which was stowed a seaplane on a catapult.

After nearly a year and 1,500 dives, everything climaxed on December 8th, 1932, when the M2 was raised to just six-metres of the surface - but suddenly, a burst of bad weather meant the operation had to be abandoned and she was sent hurtling back to the seabed.

> Everyone seemed to feel this was the 'do or die' chance. It was a day of bitter disappointment to the navy and every officer and man engaged in the operation. [42]

The task for Naafi canteen staff was considered so unusual that they were granted an extended leave pass after their efforts on the assignment.

***

Harry Banham finally made his farewells to his parents as his ambition to see the world was granted in 1927. His first stop was serving the *Shanghai Defence Force,* a unit designed to protect British business interests in China, which were being threatened by civil war. When he docked in Shanghai, Harry was surprised 'as the buildings on the river were all European style.'

Naafi had been mobilized to serve the 14,000 British troops sent to the city, and Harry was entrusted with setting up a makeshift canteen in a hut surrounded by thick rusting barbed wire in Yangtse-Pu: 'Its condition can be judged by the fact that its former occupants were Indian army mules.' It was a rigorous and tiring assignment, made worse by the fact Harry was bitten by a malaria-infected mosquito which kept him in hospital for

---

[42] Daily Mirror, December 8th, 1932.

two months. Once he had recovered, many new options for travel presented themselves. By the summer of 1930, he was serving tea to officers in the bastion of English privilege on the suburbs of Baghdad in temperatures of 122F in the shade, 'fortunately, I moved to Mosul very soon after, where things were more comfortable at 116F, because of the Kurdish hills nearby.'

Harry Banham in 1974

By the time Harry began to tolerate the Iraqi climate, the Regular Army had returned to a small, professional outfit, primarily tasked with empire policing, but, with military budgets hampered by the *Wall Street Crash,* attracting new recruits became difficult. In spite of this, Naafi business remained brisk in the UK and at their outfits in Bermuda, Ceylon, Germany, Gibraltar, Jamaica, China, Malta, and across the Middle East.

A snapshot of army life was provided by the *West London Observer* in 1930 when one of their journalists visited *Wellington Barracks* in Knightsbridge (where Trooping the Colours begins). He noted the Naafi was packed on

Friday, with it being payday, but by Tuesday though, money became tight and on Thursday 'low water' was reached:

> Roast lamb on pay-day gives place to roast mutton later in the week; fried fillet of fish becomes the homely fish cake, and instead the juicy chop and tomatoes 'Tommy' must content himself with the less expensive but just as savoury tripe and onions.

It seems even during the depression that the forces were generally appreciative of the Naafi, but there were occasions when the institute made cockeyed decisions, like in 1932 when it organised a 'toy sale' in Portsmouth. Hardly any toys were sold and the shipment was returned to London. The local newspaper advised that Naafi should avoid experimenting and blindly chasing profit with 'the sale of sidelines' in preference to concentrating its activities on the provision of everyday necessities for the Navy.

> Naafi should recognize the failure of this toy display as warning regarding having its attention is distracted from the primary purpose which it was designed to fulfil.

Just before Christmas 1934, British troops deployed to the Saar to ensure the maintenance of order during the plebiscite. The *Treaty of Versailles* had placed the area, which was formerly part of Germany, under the administration of the League of Nations for a period of 15-years. The vote resulted in an overwhelming majority in favour of a return to Germany, much to the delight of

Adolf Hitler.

Within a week of arriving in the Saar, Naafi had opened bars, restaurants and a shop in Saarbrucken and Harburg. Games, radio-sets, and books were shipped in, whilst the Naafi *Imperial Players* – a gang of entertainers specialising in 'concert parties' also performed and proved hugely popular. In all, 42 canteen staff served in the 'Saar Plebiscite Force' – where they remained until February 1935, when the region was handed to Berlin.

The following year, the German army invaded the demilitarised Rhineland but soothed international tension by captivating the world at the Berlin Olympic Games - a major triumph for the Nazi propaganda machine. Then in 1938 came the annexation of Austria, the Sudeten crisis, and the vicious November pogroms.

That same year, journalist Harry J. Greenwall went to look at the vast operations of Naafi in the Middle East. Just prior to the outbreak of war, there were seven institutes in Khartoum, and thirteen in Iraq, including a cinema. At Kenya there was one institute for the Air Force, and at Aden there were six Naafi's serving the RAF, Armoured Car sections, Wireless sections, Royal Artillery, Air headquarters, Royal Engineers and Supply sections.

In the Cairo district alone, Greenwall inspected no fewer than thirty institutes and shops and saw 'train loads of foodstuffs come up straight from the quays to the platforms erected outside the store-houses.'

He saw the Canal Zone, where there were nine institutes, and reported on Palestine where Naafi ran twenty-two institutes and shops, including a restaurant-hotel. He observed:

Of course, behind all the institutes and the cafes, and the dance halls, and the swimming baths, and the canteens, there is a vast organisation which deals with details.

The Naafi has brought out from England two or three lady assistants to give what is called a "feminine touch" to the work that Naafi is doing. They see that meals are daintily served these ladies provide a variety in menus; they arrange dances, and they see that the ices are all in order. I happened to go into a bakery which is naturally part of Naafi, and there I saw a nice tray of very enticing looking cakes just about to be sent out to the house of an officer's wife who was giving a bridge party that afternoon.

I went into shops beautifully stocked with sports accessories; the regiment can obtain its trophies, and the officers can obtain their cricket bats and their golf clubs. The men can obtain just everything they want. They are on equal terms with the officers, when it comes to Naafi.[43]

---

[43] Britannia and Eve, July 1st, 1938

CHAPTER 5
NAAFI, STEP FORWARD

BY THE autumn of 1939 sandbags were piled high outside the gates of *Imperial Court*, where an armed civilian guard peered out through a small fortified hole keeping a vigilant watch on Kennington Lane.

The building had been stripped of her luxury, and workman toiled digging an over-sized Anderson-type shelter in the courtyard, which they covered with corrugated iron. The growth of the Army and Air Force was particularly apparent across London, with the increasing number of men in uniform and constant roar of planes in the skies overhead. By September 1939, nearly two and a half million people had volunteered their time with the Territorial Army and Civil Defence.

There was no rationing or blackouts yet, but the fragile peace in Europe was unravelling. In preparation, Naafi embarked on recruiting a thousand extra men and women to fill positions as store managers, shop assistants, cooks and kitchen maids.[44]

When Hitler ordered his troops across the frontier into Poland on September 1st, the institute was as prepared as it could be, but the outlook was grim.

On Sunday 3rd September, five hundred Naafi staff poured out of the Oval tube station heeding their call-up, just as Neville Chamberlain was broadcasting the declaration of war a mile away in Downing Street. Each

---

[44] In fact, by then, Naafi had also taken responsibility for providing messes with perishable items like eggs, butter, bacon and fish, which in itself was a huge undertaking.

man had agreed that should a 'national emergency occur,' they would be willing to serve the corporation overseas. The mood was especially unusual, as the racket of kids playing was nowhere to be heard, as thousands of children had been whisked off to evacuation reception centres in the countryside.

By midday, the *Imperial Court* canteen was packed, with the air thick with tense anticipation and no little amount fear. 'The dining room of the HQ had been turned into a recruitment reception area for those of us that had been selected for posting with the *British Expeditionary Force* to France,' recalled Jimmy Howard, a club manager from RAF Dishforth. He had cause to remember this nerve wrecking experience. 'By three o'clock that afternoon, I had been attested and given the rank of Staff Quartermaster-Sergeant in charge of some sixty Naafi civilians and new recruits.' Medical and fitness tests were administered, uniforms issued and recruits ordered to report for service the following week. Naafi said they would give the same service to those on the front as it did at home: 'and will establish such institutes as may be required in whatever accommodation may be available. It will ensure that all ranks in the front line, well as at the bases, get what they need, from cigarettes to shaving soap at prices that they can afford.'[45]

Basic military training began at Mitcham, Hindhead and Croydon, whilst a dedicated Naafi facility at Norwood saw 20,000 men get their first taste of army life. Although Naafi's role was not a fighting one, they were prepared to stand shoulder-to-shoulder with their customers in the face of the enemy. At Norwood, recruits absorbed a great deal of information very quickly. They not only learned

---

[45] Gloucester Citizen, September 14th, 1939

how to use ammunition but also drilled and paraded, endured extreme physical training, were taught how to Blanco webbing and most crucially, they discovered military discipline. Few will ever forget bayonet training, when instructors bellowed: 'Whip it in, whip it out and wipe it,' as they charged toward sacks of sand. Others were astonished at the size and weight of the Lee Enfield .303 rifle, which left many men with bruised shoulders, but could shoot a bullet over 2,000 yards.

To ensure unified command, Naafi personnel serving on battlefronts fell under military control. Men were commissioned or enlisted in the Royal Army Services Corp and designated 'RASC / EFI' (Expeditionary Forces Institutes). The RASC was responsible for keeping the British Army supplied with most provisions, with the exception of arms and munitions.

Female Naafi staff, although not yet called on for overseas service, fell under the umbrella of the Auxiliary Territorial Service (ATS).[46] Such designations meant that Naafi workers overseas would be subject to military orders and discipline, whilst also being protected by the rules of the Geneva Convention.

These first recruits laid the foundation for Naafi operations in theatres of war, earning their stripes the same way as members of the military.

The situation was slightly different for shipboard

---

[46] Male EFI personnel were members of the Royal Army Service Corps until 1965, then the Royal Army Ordnance Corps. Since 1993 they have been members of the Royal Logistic Corps. Female personnel were members of the Auxiliary Territorial Service until 1949, then the Women's Royal Army Corps until 1992, when they joined the RAOC (and later the RLC).

personnel as they joined the *Naval Canteen Service* (NCS), wearing navy uniforms, but remaining ordinary civilians. The dangers of serving in the NCS were manifest: five men of the *Naval Canteen Service*—along with 515 sailors— were the first Naafi casualties, killed just two weeks after the war began, when the *HMS Courageous* was torpedoed by a German submarine.

By the time hostilities began, the NCS had mustered 26 launches for service. The ships were anything from 30 to 70 feet long and 9 to 19 feet wide across the beam. Even more were commissioned during the course of the war, including three 'Looe luggers,' two 25-tonners, the *Ruxley* and the *Claygate, Brompton, Catterick*, and *Kenning*, all laid down in 1940 and all 48 feet long, with 12 feet across the beam and 30hp Kelvin engines. They were small, but powerful and hoisted onto capital ships for redeployment in local ports.

These launches zipped between the fighting ships and Naafi stores on shore, transporting fresh produce, food and other stocks. Merchandise was sold to paymasters who resold it to the ships' company. The launches were a welcome sight for all British staffers, military and civilian alike. They operated locally from Scapa Flow, Firth of Forth, down to Weymouth Bay and Plymouth Sound, but also internationally along the Medway, Malta Harbour, the Italian and Grecian coasts, and even in Africa.

During the winter of 1939, which was the coldest for 45-years, a coxswain took a 700-mile journey to deliver a new launch from Cornwall to Scotland. His challenges included sailing through frosts and fog, then being storm-bound and trapped in ice. From all sides came the warning: 'that boat won't drown you, but she might starve you,' an allusion to the fact that by far the biggest challenge was that such rough going made cooking impossible. In addition, the boat faced enemy submarines, aircraft, and mines. Yet she braved it all. When naval authorities refused permission for the craft to proceed through a minefield, the brave seaman stated, 'She'll sail over 'em!' And so she did.

As we will see as our story develops, canteen staff didn't simply handle their official job descriptions. They were obliged to jump into a different type of action at the first sign of enemy engagement.

CHAPTER 6
NAAFI GOES TO WAR

AS NAZI forces tore through Poland, the evacuation of *Imperial Court* was underway, with the building being blacked-out and used to anchor a jovial barrage balloon which floated above. All that remained to do was for the 800 Naafi staff to move out of harm's way to their new home at *Ruxley Towers* in the countryside south of the capital.[47]

Some were oddly grateful to be leaving the dangers of London, but the process was an irritating affair as their new workplace turned out to be a claustrophobic Georgian pile. To make space, workmen threw-up a sprawling mass of huts to be used as offices, whilst nearby houses were requisitioned as billets.

While this business was going on, troops from the *British Expeditionary Force* landed in France to shore-up the French defences. They were delighted to find Naafi refreshment vans serving tea. In fact, the institute had met the challenge of opening depots in Brest and Nantes and managed to set up canteen accommodation for 40,000 men.[48]

As the war was on, but not actually being raged, British soldiers enjoyed a remarkable amount of free time. They

---

[47] The evacuation plan was devised in April, 1939. Other vital organisations to leave the capital included the *Post Office,* which moved to Harrogate, the *Bank of England* ended up in the sleepy village of Overton in Hampshire and the BBC converted an old Victorian railway tunnel near Bristol into an emergency studio.

[48] Eventually, 3,000 personnel wearing the uniforms of EFI, were serving refreshments at 230 canteens.

played football, cycled in the countryside and were taken on day trips to see the marvels of the Maginot Line.[49] By the 20th September, just two weeks since war was declared, the BEF force of some 100,000 men had settled in its concentration area.

Yet the enthusiasm seen in those first days began to fizzle, giving way to weariness as the novelty of thumb twiddling wore off. With little to do during this 'phoney war' period, many servicemen bemoaned the futility of their situation and their desire to go home.

Even star-turns like George Formby, who packed-up his ukulele to play at BEF camps for an entire month during the winter of 1940 weren't enough to ease the restlessness. But ENSA can't be accused of not trying - they also arranged 'all in wrestling' evenings, an 'all-star concert party,' and countless ropey stage productions ranging from Shakespeare to Dickens.

To make matters worse, Naafi began to struggle to cope with such a huge task – supplies frequently ran out, which could be the cause of huge flare-ups between staff and customers. Mobile canteen workers were harassed and accused of dawdling, taking crafty naps in the van and never having enough cigarettes. Occasionally, canteen staff did a spot of empathetic moaning alongside those on the other side of the counter.

The Army deployment was also beset with problems; such as when territorial units arrived in France without knives, forks, and mugs –one Tommy referred to the deployment as 'organised disorganisation'.

Anyone that has served knows armies are intensely emotional organisations. The frustrations in France lead a few men to shoot off complaints to Fleet Street, which

---

[49] Cinema shows were given in the Maginot Line itself and sports goods and newspapers were issued free to the troops.

resulted in bruising headlines such as: 'Troops at front are angry with Naafi'.[50] Whilst Naafi denied allegations of chaos and mismanagement, they could not brush off the accusations of high prices, inconsistent service and erratic availability of supplies (much of it was being pilfered at railheads, in transit and at base ports).

And with more troops pouring into France, the situation worsened, as Naafi was left chronically overextended. It continued to feverishly recruit staff, but with so many men joining the armed forces, getting suitable manpower proved almost impossible. Only the help of private contractors slightly eased the problem. One frequent moan from Tommy Atkins (slang for a common soldier in the British Army) was the price of beer. To reduce costs, a scheme was devised to brew English-style ale in France, selling it at four pence a pint, but by the time that got underway many men had discovered that French pubs were so cheap that they could 'get very drunk on two francs a night'.[51] In fact, over the course of their campaign in France, 171 BEF men were court-marshalled purely for drunkenness, many others were reprimanded.[52]

As for the Naafi, they remained under siege as philanthropic institutions made it clear they too were unhappy. The YMCA, *Church Army* and *Salvation Army* hauled the institute over the coals for having to buy supplies for sale in their establishments exclusively from Naafi. Chaplain C.B. Mortlake was so miffed he wrote: 'Compulsory buying through Naafi is also a source of grievance. I have heard, for example, that if a unit grows its own vegetable produce it must sell it to Naafi and buy

---

[50] Daily Herald, January 27th, 1940

[51] Memoirs of L.Arlington kept in the archives of the IWM London.

[52] From *The British Expeditionary Force 1939 – 1940* by Edward Smalley. AIAA; 2015

it back again at current prices.'[53]

There were also grumbles on the home front, where politician WW Wakefield, the Conservative Member of Parliament for Swindon, became one of Naafi's noisiest and most prominent critics. When soldiers wrote to him complaining about canteen prices, he held aloft two eggs in the chamber of *House of Commons* and declared: 'I don't know what the hen was that produced this egg, but it is a foreign egg and was sold in the Naafi for two pence. At a shop nearby, a British egg—you can see the difference in the size (it was bigger)—was also sold for two pence.' [54] Wakefield went on: 'I have had a number of examples of high prices and unsatisfactory service. I think there is a general feeling, particularly among the executive officers of the Naafi, that they have a monopoly, and that this causes them to adopt a sort of take-it-or-leave-it attitude.' [55]Sir Walter Venning, the Quarter Master General, agreed that the situation was quite beyond the pale. He launched a probe which concluded that Naafi had been slow to adapt to wartime conditions, ignored criticism and failed to make the institutes 'sufficiently attractive' to those using them. Another report by Sir Andrew Macharg and Lancelot Royle (prior to his appointment as chairman) was more sympathetic, acknowledging 'Naafi management had been strained almost to breaking point

---

[53] Shields Daily News, August 7th, 1940

[54] Daily Mirror, March 8th, 1940

[55] Air Estimates, House of Commons debate March 7th, 1940. WW Wakefield MP: "I should like the Under-Secretary, together with the other Departments concerned, to have an inquiry made into the running of this body (Naafi). It seems to be an independent body under nobody's rule or guidance. It has a monopoly and it is not discharging its duties in the way that it ought to do." Wakefield also remarked: "I think that one reason for the lack of proper service is to be found in the long hours and underpayment of those who have to provide the service."

and that staff of military age had been snatched by the armed forces.'[56]

By early summer 1940, Naafi had just managed iron out most of their existing problems in France when some disturbing news arrived.

---

[56] From *Service to the Services* by Harry Miller, 1970. Pages 51 -52.

CHAPTER 7
DUNKIRK

THE 'phoney war' came to an abrupt end on May 10th 1940 when a lightning German strike through the Ardennes split the Allied forces in two, eventually leaving the British hemmed in along the coast near Dunkirk.

There was little to inspire confidence when stranded soldiers tuned-into the distant signals of the BBC to hear newly appointed Prime Minister Winston Churchill ordering their immediate withdrawal from the continent.

Like everyone else, the three-thousand EFI workers beat a hasty retreat to avoid falling into the jaws of the German army, abandoning trucks, cars, and tons of stock in the process. In the midst of the chaos, there are tales of EFI men performing amazing juggling acts of retreat and devotion to duty.[57] Some canteen managers 'staggered into reception depots with account books and familiar black boxes containing the takings in francs to a total value of several hundred thousand pounds.'[58] Naafi officer Claude Luke observed:

> At the time when the military situation was growing more confused every hour, when the Army was commandeering all available transport, and when the rumour and panic had already seized the civilian population and sent them out in frenzied columns upon the traffic choked-highways. The order went forth to all EFI units:

---

[57] It was estimated that Naafi lost over one million pounds worth of goods.
[58] According to Harry Miller's 1970 book *Service to the Services*.

men, money and books and, stocks were to be saved – in that sequence.[59]

An abandoned Naafi canteen tent in France, occupied by German soldiers. (Authors private collection).

Abandoned stock sometimes ended up in British hands, as Harry Hargreaves a sailor aboard *H.M.S. Fernie* recalled. His ship was charged with picking up stragglers near Cherbourg. 'Words of mine can never convey fully the scene that faced us... as far as the eye could see was a graveyard of vehicles of every kind. Bren gun carriers, troop transports, supply vehicles, ambulances, motorbikes, canteen trucks, army coloured automobiles, even bicycles.' But, Hargreaves added, there was a silver lining that day as the crew spotted fully loaded Naafi vans

---

[59] Claude Luke, Daily Telegraph, October, 1940

abandoned by the road. 'Naturally [the sailors] made a beeline for these and our canteen manager was furious. He knew it would be a long time before he sold any more cigarettes or chocolate.'

Between May 27th and June 4th, more than 330,000 men made it home during *Operation Dynamo* onboard small ships, private yachts, and fishing boats - transforming the disaster into a victory of sorts. The Admiralty had called on the public to help with the evacuation, making an appeal during a broadcast on May 14th:

> The Admiralty have made an order requesting all owners of self-propelled pleasure craft between 30ft and 100ft in length to send all particulars to the Admiralty within 14 days from today if they have not already been offered or requisitioned.

News that so many Tommies managed to wade through waters to little rescue ships during that dramatic evacuation was hailed by Churchill as a 'miracle of deliverance' and enabled the Allies to continue fighting.

But, the story didn't end there. Over 150,000 others remained stranded on the continent, prompting *Operation Ariel*—the final evacuation of Allied forces. In one attempt, thousands of soldiers, along with a small number of civilian refugees, gathered at the port of Saint-Nazaire to board the *Lancastria* on June 17, the same day that France capitulated to Germany's terms of surrender.

The docks were crammed with noise, as buses rattled to the embarkation points and military policemen screamed instructions as they attempted to keep order during the chaos. 400 EFI men, along with their salvaged stock, had already boarded the *Lancastria* that morning. Because of her immense size, she was anchored 5 miles offshore - so small tenders were required to ferry passengers and cargo out to her. On board, space was so tight, with decks crammed full of soldiers clutching their rifles as civilians held onto bags, packages, and small suitcases.

With embarkation completed at noon, the ship was filled beyond capacity. Among the 6,000 troops, were airmen, employees of British companies, and staff from the *Church Army, Salvation Army*, and YMCA. Captain Rudolf Sharp received permission to sail at 2.15pm, but concerned about the possibility of German U-boats striking, he decided to wait for a Royal Navy escort. This proved to be a catastrophic error, as Sharp's 550-ft long vessel became a sitting target for the Luftwaffe - at 3.45pm – an hour and a half after she could have sailed - eight German Stuka attackers moved in for the kill.

As the German planes approached, passengers screamed and climbed over each other in search of safety. Under heavy bombardment, the scene descended into chaos.

Her fate was sealed when the boiler room took a direct hit, followed by hits fore, aft, and to the funnel. James Cockburn from the BEF was onboard:

> By this time the ship began to list badly on one side and the crew were trying hard to get the men onto the other side in order to right itself but this didn't last long. Slowly the ship began to sink — bow first. Men were jumping overboard in panic; others on the upper decks were throwing anything floatable into the water, but instead of helping these objects were landing on the men's heads knocking them out.[60]

---

[60] WW2 Peoples War, BBC. Article ID: A4307447

Within twenty minutes she had rolled onto her port side and slid beneath the waves. EFI Sergeant Geoffrey William Singleton managed to escape the hulk, recalling 'a number of men stayed on the ship until she finally sank.' Singletons daughter Diana Clarke recounts how her father went up onto the deck to get a cup of tea, a decision which saved his life: 'He was able to jump into the sea and swim, eventually being picked up by a French fishing vessel. He lost many friends.'

Petty Officer Frank Clements, with the *Naval Canteen Service*, was on a nearby vessel and frantically tried to locate as many survivors as possible. 'He did all he could,' his brother Arthur remembered, 'he even pulled a little baby out of the sea.' Many soldiers had been ordered not to abandon their rifles; Clements screamed at them to let go of their guns, many of the soldiers would not - and perished.

Singleton later recalled, 'a number of men stayed on the ship until it finally sank. They were singing *There'll Always Be an England* and *Roll out the Barrel*.' With the *Lancastria* beneath the waves, German planes returned to machine-gun what was left, killing scores of men clinging to a raft.

More than 3,000 lives were lost that day. It constituted the biggest loss of life on a single ship in British maritime history and left Winston Churchill so shocked that he banned details of the tragedy being reported. In all, Naafi's lost 109 men at Dunkirk and 57 were taken prisoner. In France, an exhausted Marshal Petain, the 84-year-old Premier, said the 'cause of our defeat' was 'too few children, too few arms, too few allies.'

When weary evacuees landed in Britain, Naafi were on duty operating makeshift restaurants in over 800 marquees, and handing out ration-packs to exhausted men.

***

Good news from the seas was scant. Eight months before Dunkirk, a German U-boat fired two torpedoes at the battleship *HMS Royal Oak* moored at Scapa Flow in Scotland, debunking the belief that the huge natural harbour was safe from enemy fire. Within eight minutes of the second torpedo striking, the *Royal Oak* began shaking and tilting, then it suddenly shifted over and slowly began to sink. There were desperate scenes as rescue workers scrambled to reach the stricken ship. She went under just 13 minutes after the second strike, with the loss of 833 men, including Rear-Admiral Henry Blagrove, commander of the Second Battle Squadron.

Naval Canteen Superintendent George Rogers and his colleague Henry Martin sprang into action, opening shop on Scapa Pier for the use of emergency landing parties. Naafi boats—including *The Scarlet Thread*—helped rescue seamen and retrieve the dead, including the body of *The Royal Oak* canteen manager. Rogers later recalled that night:

> …in the inky blackness and deathly silence of the early morning the few people gathered on the pier could only peer into the impenetrable darkness straining their eyes to see movement and listening for the sound of returning boats. All lights, oil stoves, and heating apparatus available were lighted and waiting in our depot in a short time, and blankets were laid out ready for survivors.[61]

---

[61] From *Naafi in Uniform* by Howard N.Cole. The Forces Press. Page 136.

A month later, the first major naval engagement took place when the *HMS Exeter* spotted the German battleship *Admiral Graf Spee* in the South Atlantic.

Luckily, two other British ships the *HMS Ajax* and the *HMS Achilles* were nearby. 'Action stations at the double' sounded, but the German ship had already seen the British and initiated battle with three salvoes, starting with fire on *HMS Exeter*.

All British seamen, including canteen staff, rushed to their battle stations. The *Exeter's* canteen first assistant helped in the medical party and soon after the first shots were fired, injured men started filling the infirmary. An-11 inch shell hit the ship from below, impacting the area where most NCS members were working. They were knocked down and had to contend with fumes and smoke choking them.

'When I came to my senses,' a canteen manager later said recalling the incident, 'the place was in complete darkness.' He went on:

> I managed to reach the bulkhead door leading to fresh air. A minute later someone came through the smoke and it turned out to be my youngest assistant. We rushed into the open air together. I then noticed the lad had been burnt on his arm, leg, and forehead. His hair was singed. We ran along the deck, pulled a fire hose along the deck, and helped a couple of the crew to put out a fire. By this time the ship was a shambles. Just after, I saw my other assistant, and was relieved to know he was safe.

He spoke of the close bond between the NCS men and navy, as they faced hours of chaos, danger and fighting.

Scores of men were injured, including two canteen assistants. Many died too, and were subsequently buried at sea. Although still seaworthy, after putting up an extraordinary fight with the *Admiral Graf Spee*, the *Exeter* was badly damaged. It still retired with pride, flying the White Ensign on a broken mast.

After the fight, the canteen manager recalled:

> I saw my first assistant, and found he was uninjured. He had done some very good work tending the wounded. The next thing was to see how 'our department' had fared in the action. The canteen wasn't touched, but the soda fountain was, as an 11-inch shell exploded nearby. I next inspected our storeroom. On opening the hatch I found it was flooded with oil fuel and water. After it had been pumped out we found we had to give all the stores to *Father Neptune*.

The *Admiral Graf Spee* next focused on the *Ajax*. Despite having a mainmast shot away, the *Ajax* managed to get within 8,000 yards of the enemy, a distance close enough that the crew could shoot torpedoes. The Germans, however, also took advantage of the distance and the *Admiral Graf Spee* scored a direct hit with an 11inch gun. Luckily the British ships managed to exert enough damage on the German ship. Canteen staffers were part of it all. Those involved included canteen manager Henry Kirkham, who helped administer first aid, G.C. Addley and W. King, who assisted the 6inch gun ammunition party, as well as K.E. Rands and G.A. Ivers, who did their part in the 4inch gun supply team. Rands was part of the team firing the first rounds. Their hard work paid off and the *Graf Spee* limped into Montevideo port, but neutral

Uruguay gave in to British pressure and sent it back out on November 15th. Captain Langsdorf, the commander of the *Graf Spee*, protested bitterly against the Uruguayan Government's decision, complaining he needed more time to make the necessary repairs to his damaged warship, especially the kitchens and bakery.

That night at 7pm, the final stage of the battle was played out.

Despite the parlous state of the *Graf Spee,* she left Montevideo travelling to the River Plate. British ships were at full alert - but their guns were no longer necessary. The *Graf Spee* was scuttled—blowing herself up—in the harbour's entrance.

Basking in this moment of victory, a canteen staff member said it was 'a sight never to be forgotten.'

THE NAAFI STORY

CHAPTER 8
THE HOME FRONT

The summer of 1940 was strange, to say the least. With the Nazi jackboot marching across much of Europe, many people in Britain were left terrified at the prospect of a German invasion. Such fears worsened on July 16th, when Hitler lifted his gigantic blaze secrecy on the issue and declared: 'As England, in spite of the hopelessness of her military position, has so far shown herself unwilling to come to any compromise, I have decided to begin to prepare for, and if necessary to carry out, an invasion of England.'

His threat arrived six-weeks after Dunkirk. In London, the government had already been busy suppressing news of the *Lancastria* disaster, after a multitude of setbacks had made the public vulnerable, as British fortunes sank to their lowest ebb.

But, even faced with such a perilous situation, the re-emergence of the good old British stiff-upper-lip was noted at many Naafi canteens, where a new raft of jokes made the rounds.

> *It is feared in some quarters that if many more German planes are brought down in this country the Anti-litter Society will resign bloc.*

> *A famous German artist on his way to Rome. It seems his great ambition is do still-life study of the Italian Navy.*

In fact, with morale at a premium, Naafi was called upon to try and cheer things up. Under the chairmanship of Sir Seymour Hicks, the newly created *Entertainment National Service Association* – known as ENSA - was established to arrange live performances for the forces. The unit fell directly under Naafi control, with theatrical producer Basil Dean overseeing a vast portfolio of actors, comics, musicians, and administrators. Much has been written about ENSA over the years, and rightly so, as it chalked up some remarkable achievements and helped to launch the careers of countless performers. The outfit began in a back office at *Imperial Court*, but then moved to the *Royal Theatre* on Drury Lane, from where the services of popular entertainers including Leslie Banks, Robert Donat, and Dame Sybil Thorndike were secured. Its early days were recorded by Claude Luke in the *Royal United Services Institution Journal.*

> As soon as war appeared inevitable, Mr. Basil Dean, who for some months had been working on a scheme for the organization of professional entertainers in war-time, was appointed Director of Entertainments for Naafi. Not an hour was lost in adapting it for its urgent mission. At the outset, the entire organization comprised of six men and a theatre. A skeleton staff was engaged and augmented week by week. The historic dressing rooms (at Drury Lane) were rapidly stripped and equipped as offices. Sir Seymour Hicks moved into the room where Sheridan wrote *School for Scandal.*

Within a year, ENSA had become the largest

entertainments organisation in Britain, surpassing even the BBC - with 25,000 live performances and 14,000 cinema shows completed between September 1939 and August 1940. As noted earlier, even before Dunkirk, ENSA had chalked-up 5420 shows for the BEF in France.

One thing is certain, the home-troops and war workers were not starved of entertainment, as ENSA arranged shows for the dockers in Liverpool and special 'munitions concerts' at factories was provided by fifty touring concert parties, starring Vic Oliver, Evelyn Laye, Arthur Askey, Frances Day, Pat Kirkwood, Florence Desmond, Flanagan and Allen, Naunton Wayne and Billy Bennett.

The unit even had its own song titled: 'We Must All Stick Together' which introduced all shows. It was written and composed by Ralph Butler and Raymond Wallace, and was brought to the controller of ENSA by Noel Gay, of 'Lambeth Walk' fame.

We must all stick together.
All stick together.
Never mind the old school tie, United we shall stand.
Whatever may befall, The richest in the land.
The poorest of us all; We must all stick together.
Birds of a feather.
And the clouds will soon roll by.

Cheery songs could not alter the growing sense of morbid gloom sweeping across a landscape of taped windows, rations, blackouts and air-raid shelters. The prices of butter, eggs, livestock, meat, potatoes and milk had already been fixed as part of a complete re-planning of food supplies. Half of the meat in the UK and most of the bacon, butter and sugar was imported from overseas. For the grumblers, and there were plenty of them, the Ministry of Food published four reasons for planned rationing in all newspapers.[62]

- **RATIONING PREVENTS WASTE OF FOOD** We must not ask our sailors to bring us unnecessary food cargoes at the risk of their lives.

- **RATIONING INCREASES OUR WAR EFFORT** Our shipping carries food, and armaments in their raw and finished state, and other essential raw materials for home consumption and the export trade. To reduce our purchases of food abroad is to release ships for bringing us other imports. So we shall strengthen our war effort.

- **RATIONING DIVIDES SUPPLIES EQUALLY** There will be ample supplies for our 44 million people, but we must divide them fairly, everyone being treated alike. No one must be left out.

---

[62] Herbert Morrison, the Food Minister, was in favour of immediate rationing but was overruled by the War Cabinet in November, 1939. Sir Samuel Hoare, Lord Privy Seal, rejected any demands for comprehensive rationing as being 'quite unnecessary,' saying it would be a gift to German propaganda.

- **RATIONING   PREVENTS UNCERTAINTY** Your Ration Book assures you of your fair share. Rationing means that there will be no uncertainty.

When meat rationing began in early 1940, there was acute relief that liver, kidney, tripe, heart, ox-tail, poultry and game could be bought without coupons. Sausages, meat pies and galantines (containing not more than 50 percent meat) were not rationed either and coupons were not required for meat served by canteens (including Naafi and the *British Restaurants*), schools, and catering establishments — which were all rationed at the sources of supply.

The Ministry of Food also told the public: 'When you cannot get imported beef, bear in mind that our fighting Forces, whose needs must come first, consume a large proportion of our supplies. Remember that the eating of home-killed instead of imported meat saves shipping space and foreign exchange.'

Naafi made sure they did their bit too. Staff dreamt up a selection of 'reliable wartime recipes' advising cooks to eke out the most from the limited amount of meat available. One suggestion, with liver and kidneys un-rationed, was to prepare the fancy sounding 'Liver a la Francais' – which was basically liver and onions in gravy.

Other suggestions, including *Sausage Pie, Vegetable Pie, Cheese Pudding* and *Sugarless Cake* tested well initially, but never sold and were soon ditched from menus. Other ideas for filling and yet sustaining menus were churned out by Mr. TA Laton in the *Imperial Club Magazine*. Some of his creative menus - like the 'cheap sandwich' - sounded beyond ropey:

Here is a really cheap sandwich and much tastier than it sounds: it doesn't really need any butter. Use any tinned fish of the sardine type – herring, brisling, sardine, sild, either in oil or tomato. Cut the tails off and mash them up and DON'T forget to mash in every drop of oil and tomato juice. Now use up that bit of cheese you were about to throw away and mash this in with the fish, adding a good dollop of pepper; instead of butter. You may have a drop of bottled mayonnaise you cannot use, so spread this in thinly on the bread and put on the mixture. And remember, it tastes better than it sounds.

Mr. Laton's tips ended abruptly when *Imperial Club Magazine* ceased publication in mid-1940 due to an acute paper shortage, but advice continued via the pages of the *Health for All Magazine*, where another example of wartime economy included a drink 'costing nothing' which could be made by boiling water on the skins and pips of oranges, lemons and grapefruit and allowing it to stand a few hours and then strain.

Unusual foodstuffs began to appear in the shops, such as whale meat and tinned snoek fish from South Africa – and, even though they were not rationed, they weren't popular either.

As well as receiving a welter of pamphlets advising them how to work with rationing, cooks were also given fuel economy instructions, like the order to cease all fires in all institutes, except for cooking purposes, during the summer months. In many canteens electricity consumption was cut down by reducing 100 watt lamps to 60 or 40 watt bulbs. Staff were also told to cook 'hot oven' pastries in the mornings and use less heat for biscuits and buns in the afternoons.

The possibility of hunger and food insecurity became a major concern during the late 1930s. Just before the war, the *University of Cambridge* conducted an experiment to find out whether Britain could survive with only domestic food production in the event of German submarines cutting-off all imports. Researchers fed themselves one egg, one pound of meat and four ounces of fish per week; one-quarter pint of milk a day; four ounces of margarine; and unlimited amounts of potatoes, vegetables and wholemeal bread. Several weeks of intensive outdoor exercise simulated the arduous wartime physical work Britons would likely have to perform. The scientists found that the subjects' health and performance remained very good after three months, but a 'remarkable' increase in flatulence from the high amount of starch in the diet was recorded. They also noted that their faeces had increased by 250 percent in volume.

Starch provided the backbone of menus at new *British Restaurants* – which were created in 1941 to provide cheap meals – patrons included bombed-out families, as well as factory workers. Customers entered through a barrier, purchased food tickets and then either left with their meal in their own containers, or ate in the restaurant using crockery and cutlery provided. Tea was served at a penny a cup and each table seated about 12 people.

However, soon after the restaurants began popping up, cutlery theft became endemic. At a branch in Horsforth, the manager carped that her establishment was 'being disgracefully abused' by 'cutlery crooks'. She was so insanely irritated that printed cards were placed on the tables drawing attention to the disappearance of knives, forks, and spoons offering a reward for information leading to the detection of the thieves.

The situation was just as bad in Leeds, where a canteen worker was fed up with finding replacements: 'If the taking of cutlery doesn't stop, then either people will have to bring their own or use their fingers.' The dilemma had driven her staff mad with frustration and rage.

Another civilian scheme: *Digging for Victory* utilized waste ground, railway sidings, ornamental gardens and lawns for farming or vegetable growing.

Thankfully, Naafi girls weren't required to do much digging. In fact, newsreels sought to glamorize and elevate them to boost recruitment, but their workload of dishing out hot tea by the gallon, cooking, washing up and scrubbing ovens could be backbreaking.

***

The heart of every military camp was the Naafi, and its employees were drawn from all across the country and scattered-out at big stations and rural outfits – many of which were miles away from civilisation.

Local workers were common too - within the Naafi structure - personal recommendation was the norm.

A canteen manager that needed more staff would usually start by asking around her own family and employees. It wasn't unusual for mothers and daughters to be working on the same counter, especially on some of the more remote garrisons.

The key to success were these small teams of Managers and Assistant Managers, women and men, who had the day to day responsibility of providing the highest standards of service in bars, cafeterias and shops.

For many girls, Naafi was their first time away from home and their first experience of paid work. On arrival at their new posts, they were issued white overalls for cooks, blue for canteen assistants and cotton khaki uniform for 'walking out' in.

'It was a hard and austere life,' remembered JD Wright, an 18-year-old trainee cook stationed at a barrage balloon centre in rural south Devon. When she joined Naafi in 1940, the living quarters were rough and simple, but uniforms, food, and lodgings were free, and pay was £1 a week. There was no contract to serve for the duration, and there was annual leave with pay, half-holidays and regular off-duty hours. Accommodation usually meant shacking up with five other girls in a corrugated Nissen hut, which could be testing, especially during storms when the deafening sound of the rain hitting the metal roofs drove some insane.

During winters – notably that of 1939-40- the bone-chilling cold left many girls shivering or sharing a bed in an attempt to keep warm. Rhoda Woodward will never forget arriving at her first posting in 1942 when she was issued with a cap, overalls, sheets and blankets and told to make her bed. 'I was rather dubious when I found that it had lost a leg. It was propped up with a biscuit tin, but tins were tins in those days and it did the job.'[63]

For some girls, the simpler, healthier life on rural camps was bliss, whilst others found it sorely trying. Endless chores dominate the memory of JD Wright, who discovered she needed a broad range of skills as there was always a lot of work to be done. Her days started by shunting crate loads of rock buns, jam puffs and Nelson Squares from coal-fired ovens into the canteen. Teenager Eve Diett was posted to a camp in Denbury and still clearly remembers the most horrible part of the job –

---

[63] BBC, WW2 People's War. Article ID: A4001897. May 4th, 2005. Contributed to the BBC by Ian Billingsley, author of 'Girls on the Home Front'.

which took place before the roller shutters of the canteen had even opened.

> When I had to clean the flue, I put a tea cloth wrapped around my head — wearing an old overall. There was soot everywhere, so I was always pretty black by the time the job was done, as I had to stick my arm and hands in it to move it around. You could only see the whites of my eyes because it was so dirty. I had a little spade to shovel the soot out, and that took ages. Then it had to be moved to a special dustbin…but we all had to do it.[64]

Soon after, 'gunfire,' the nickname for tea, was served from a large aluminium urn on wheels, in an attempt to rouse the soldiers. It was said if the hot water didn't work in the barrack wash-house; men would sometimes use the tea to shave.

For JD Wright, the long working day beginning at 7.30am - when all floors were scrubbed, breakfast served and counters stocked - remains etched in her memory. 'Two girls took turns to clean out the kitchen ranges and light up ready for baking cakes and heating water for the tea-urns, in time for opening the canteen at 10.30am for the Airmen's morning break.'

Eve Diett managed to work her breakfast routine out to a fine art. 'I used to have a wash, get my teeth cleaned, get back to the billet to dress and sort my hair, then dash to the kitchen and set the tables.'

Toiling behind the counter at Hornchurch aerodrome; an RAF station used for the protection of London, Mary

---

[64] Interview with author Nathan Morley, August 2018.

Thurlow discovered the 'secret technique' to making a cup of the famed Naafi char: 'They put so much tea into a big cylinder, but then they would add bicarbonate of soda to make it stronger, so they could dilute it. The head cook used to do that so we didn't see.'[65] In a wartime pamphlet, Naafi informed kitchen workers that: 'The tea leaf only yields its best when subjected to water at boiling point. i.e. bubbling fiercely ...'

Staff became expert at cooking with evaporated and dry skimmed milk, along with dehydrated eggs and potatoes; and five-pound tins of powdered soups, which when reconstituted, could make 25 gallons of liquid soup. Most of the eggs came from dehydration plants in Canada, Australia and, the United States. A pound of dried eggs expanded to the equivalent of three dozen eggs in shell. Eve Diett found the *Ministry of Food* assertion that it was 'hard to detect' the difference between powdered and the real-thing absurd. 'You get that dry taste – it's like if you put custard powder in your mouth. I used to 'doctor it' and add a bit of sauce, before putting it on bread. Whoever said shelled and powered eggs tasted the same should have eaten a mouthful.'

Rachael Foster, who was serving with *Women's Auxiliary Air Force* at Bletchley Park, the top-secret home of the code-breakers, cottoned on to the fact that Naafi tea was always stronger without sugar. Foster also remembered a favourite Naafi dinner among the code-breakers was an unusual concoction called toasted spam, 'which was a mixture of bits of ham squeezed together – that was our greatest joy.'

Mary Thurlow often served officers, pilots and rear gunners, many returning from fighting in the skies above

---

[65] It was 14 miles from London and home to RAF Fighter Command's 11 Group.

southern England. 'They used to come into the Naafi in the evening. I could see when I went to pick up cups their exhaustion – sheer exhaustion...you'd see them flop in the armchairs and sleep.'

RAF servicemen being served tea at their base in Oakington, 1944

Nora Neale was at Trumpington and will never forget her training, which 'lasted long enough to be shown how to make potato pastry for savoury flans!' The girls also gathered a basic stock of remedies for customers suffering after 'one too many.' Cures ranged from hot Bovril, cold black coffee and bitter almonds to a plate of fried eggs.

One of Nora's friends was stationed at RAF Duxford at the same time as aviator Douglas Bader and his squadron: 'When she went out on the mobile canteen she served them. Bader used to think his 'boys' should come first, but each squadron was served in rotation, so each had a 'first.' Marjorie Bodman was working at Skellingthorpe, an aerodrome under the control of RAF Bomber Command.

> For the men working on the airfield loading up the bombs on the planes ready for take-off, we had a caravan to take them their tea and cakes. The caravan was towed by a tractor, (driven by an airman) and two girls sat on the mudguards as we travelled round the aerodrome. I liked to be chosen to do this as it was nice to be in the fresh air. Many girls didn't want to as if it was windy; it upset their hair-do. Skellingthorpe was known for its woods and the bomb store was well hidden. We heard the planes take off at night and counted them in, in the early morning when we felt the bumps as they landed.[66]

Pilots were provided with 'marching chocolate,' a special Naafi variety produced to meet the demand of bomber and fighter crews in their special rations. It had been feared their supply would curtailed because of a reduction in quantity available, but this never happened.

When the girls weren't serving, they prepared rations for air crews, and even tackled the cooking of non-British dishes for Polish and other Allied troops, in an age when little was known about what was often referred to as 'foreign muck'. At some canteens, exotic spicy Indian food, including 'chupatties' was prepared – India, incidentally, was the only part of the Empire where Naafi did not operate.

Lunch was served between 1pm and 2pm, and suppers –

---

[66] BBC, WW2 People War, Article ID: A2907605. August 10th, 2004

usually consisting of pies, chops or egg and bacon with chips - began at 6pm till 10.30 pm.

One terrifying aspect of the work was the scramble to safety when the air-raid siren sounded. One girl recorded: 'We closed down the ranges, put the food on top of the ovens and went to the shelters. If it was only a short raid, we popped everything back in the ovens and carried on as normal.'

At a canteen in Wiltshire, May Aylesbury, seldom tired of telling her colleagues of her personal experience of having served Winston Churchill. Her co-workers ribbed-her into sending her story to the newspapers, which to everyone's amazement, was published. Readers learned that Mr. Churchill usually woke-up to half a cold partridge, bacon fried till it curled; a boiled egg, toast and marmalade, buttered scones and tea. [67]

Even though such trivial revelations now seem comical, a drive to foil Nazi agents saw a security officer visiting Naafi stations to 'educate employees about the kind of secrets the enemy wanted know' and how enemy agents work. As well as being told that figures relating to Tommy's cup of tea and cake were 'food for thought' to enemy agents, Naafi girls were reminded:

> A typist working on figures of messing and canteen supplies has knowledge she must never refer to outside the office. She might tell her boyfriend at a cinema about the long list of stores needed at a certain port on a particular date, not realising that the man next to her might be waiting for that knowledge to confirm the rumours he had heard that things were going to

[67] Aylesbury was employed by Ronald Tree the MP for Market Marborough, at whose home Churchill came to stay.

happen at that port. Naafi staff must realise that the agent- might not be in uniform.

Naafi girls may not have been gossips, but they were certainly more 'marriage-inclined' than any other wartime service. By the third year of the war, it was estimated that 2,500 girls were tying the knot annually. Miss RHH Crichton – 'a big woman, with dark twinkling eyes and a ready sense of humour' - was the Chief Superintendent of the Women's Section of Naafi. Her motto was: 'Hard work hurts nobody. It is worry that kills. Learn never to worry'.

By March 1942, Crichton had racked up 25-years service with the institute and had 33,209 girls under her control, with an extra 500 new recruits being added every week. She said the bridegrooms were nearly always men from the three Services, 'a girl who loves a soldier of sailor is the one who serves him with his nice cup of tea as his mother makes,' she opined.

While Naafi had not sent any women abroad during the war, a great many of them serving at home on camps, airfields and at coastal stations were in the front line. Most of the girls in the London area bunked down in air-raid shelters or slit-shelters during the Blitz.

'The camaraderie and thought for each other was something that kept everyone going in those situations,' JD Wright remembered.

In one such incident in May 1941, the Naafi club at RAF Waddington in Lincolnshire was hit by German bombs, with falling debris and fire killing a number of Naafi workers including the manageress, Constance Raven. Then, in July 1941, ten people, including six WAAFs were killed when a Hudson bomber collided with a telegraph pole and then crashed into Naafi canteen in Northern

Ireland. Three of the victims were members of the Hudson's crew, and one, an RAF ground staff member. From these awful conditions, many heart-warming tales of bravery and generosity emerged, like the time when manageress Elsie Mullin dealt with a catastrophic situation after a stick of bombs destroyed her canteen injuring many people. Covered in dust, blood and badly bruised, she stayed in the wrecked building refusing to take shelter till she had tended the wounded. Mullin was one of a dozen staff commended by the organisation at a ceremony in 1942 for the fortitude she displayed in the face of air attacks.

The same event highlighted 'conspicuous gallantry or meritorious service during air raids'. The audience heard how Henry Ford, at a naval canteen, pulled-out casualties from a wrecked building while high-explosive bombs fell near.

***

Whilst there were many heart-warming stories about Naafi on the home front, an equal number of disturbing incidents were coming to light.

In the first year of the war, the rapid growth of the organisation had piled pressure on staff and resources, prompting the appointment of one of the finest retail executives in the country. Lancelot C. Royle, formerly of *Unilever and Home & Colonial Stores*, took his position as chairman of the board of management in February 1941. On his first day, the corridors of *Ruxley Towers* buzzed with chatter about the intensive German bombing of Swansea, which had devastated the town the night before. Despite the tumult around him, Royle projected calmness from his office overlooking the lush Surrey countryside.

From there, he supervised 4,000 branches, staffed by 35,000 workers.

Royle was known as was a quick-thinking character – which wasn't surprising given he was a former army sprint champion, who had represented Great Britain as a member of the *Chariots of Fire* team in the 1924 Olympics.

Soon after his appointment, he embarked on a lightning tour of Naafi establishments. This remarkable feat - during the height of war – included 17 days of flying and five days in a ship, which took him to Bermuda, New York, Honolulu, Midway Island, Wake Island, Guam, Singapore, Rangoon, Delhi, Baghdad, Cairo, and Malta. One newspaper remarked:

> An English businessman with his bowler hat, umbrella and despatch case has just completed a round the world trip - a tribute to the British and American rule of the world's airways.

As chairman, Royle made a series of swift and canny reforms, one of the first being to give small producers the chance to sell to Naafi and introducing measures to cut the massive amount of waste.

What Royle had little control over was theft. The pilfering of food, cigarettes, chocolate and other supplies was so rampant that it was impossible to calculate the extent of losses. But with over 1.7billion cigarettes being smoked in Britain every week, in addition to over a billion shipped monthly to troops overseas through Naafi, warehouses, canteens, docks, shops and storage facilities became a source of rich-pickings, as the underworld 'did their bit' for the war effort.

Some heists were thought and planned with all the gusto that goes into more legitimate profiteering. One such occasion saw thieves raiding a Naafi warehouse at Reigate, and then making use of the electric conveyor belt to move their loot from the stores to a waiting lorry, before driving off with a million cigarettes.

Newspapers from the period are larded with reports of minor cases, such as the time four privates from the *Lincolnshire Regiment* were jailed for nabbing 360,000 cigarettes and seven bottles of whisky from a Naafi grocery store. Like many of their comrades-in-arms, the privates were caught trying to palm off their ill-gotten gains to undercover police officers.

When a Naafi driver was handed down six months' hard labour for stealing cigarettes in Derby, the sentencing judge reprimanded him severely, saying, 'The troops were entitled to think that they had the civilian population behind them.' Then there was the case of John Firth, a Naafi manager from London who was collared after promising knock-off whisky to various nightclub owners. Firth took advance payments to secure orders before disappearing. One of his victims was the owner of the famous *Windmill Club* in Old Burlington Street, who was so angry at being conned that he reported the crime to police—an unusual course of action, given that he had shelled out hundreds of pounds for contraband booze. When he was finally caught, Firth was sent down for five years of penal servitude.

Then there was the gang that broke into the Naafi canteen in the *Tower of London*, making off with cigarettes and ransacking the premises – it was possibly the only time in history when someone had tried to break into the fortress. 'The fact that the thieves were able to avoid the sentries at the Tower has led the police to believe that the robbery was a very carefully planned one. The War Office stated that it appeared to be an 'outside job.'

At a certain point, theft became so rampant that Naafi took to packing consignments of leather boots in separate cases—one for the right foot and the other for the left. 'The drawback to the division of pairs of boots is that if one case is stolen, the other is useless to us,' an official admitted, adding that 'at least the thieves gain nothing, and it acts as a deterrent.'

Even staff dormitories were not immune to thieves' sticky fingers, as was the case at Whittington Barracks, which was targeted three times in a fortnight. There, staff quarters were ransacked, with jewellery, clothing, money, glasses, sheets, blankets, and other bed linen among the stolen items.

In another case, a Naafi inspector from Hatfield was sentenced to a month behind-bars and a £50 fine for hoarding 666 tins of sausages, fruit and sardines, along with 444 chocolate bars, 200 meat cubes, dried fruits, salmon, sugar, 36 boxes of cheese and several crates of soup powder in his spare bedroom. Justices called him 'the perfect glutton' and considered the fact that he could obtain excessive supplies, while many people could not get sufficient to live on, indicated a lot of laxity in the administration of Naafi.

A month to the day after the war ended, Naafi offered the unusually high amount of £500 for the capture of the crooks that tied up a night watchman and bludgeoned a driver, before making-off with two-million cigarettes from a warehouse in Watford. At the time, the reward was biggest offered in the crime world in years—Naafi said the figure was so large because they regarded the theft as the meanest ever. The *Daily Mirror* followed the story:

The clocks had just chimed quarter past midnight when one or more lorries drew up outside the Naafi warehouse. Several men got inside, and though 63-year-old Waller Smith, the night watchman, who has served Naafi for twenty-three years, struggled to raise the alarm, they grabbed him and trussed him up. They went through the building and came across a Naafi driver, 27-year-old William Potton. He, too, put up a fight but was bludgeoned. Then the thieves—there were more than four—loaded the heavy cases on the lorries and vanished.

CHAPTER 9
NORTH, SOUTH AND EAST

COLD, rugged and alive with weather, the Mediterranean island of Crete was an uninviting place in November 1940. Sitting just 100 miles from Italy's strongholds in the Dodecanese, the jittery Greek government begged London to send troops and occupy the island to forestall an Italian occupation.

Tensions had been high in Athens when Mussolini started threatening Greece in the hope of raising fresh trouble to distract Allied attention in the Mediterranean. That, coupled with the fact that Crete dominated Italy's sea routes to Libya and Syria, added to the irritation of the island sitting in the path of Italian ships attempting to navigate the Aegean Sea.

At the outset of the British disembarkation in Crete, flights of enemy aircraft appeared and attacked the cruisers landing the troops. The sea was writhing, heaving and steadily getting choppier – but, superb seamanship ensured the landings succeeded.

After this baptism of fire, the new arrivals realized that their situation was far from ideal. Through a combination of poor planning and bad luck, British, Cypriot, and Palestinian troops were badly equipped, lightly-armed and were only provided a basic means of transport - donkey being the preferred method of movement.

Even by the time the British had set up permanent camp, Crete continued to feel insecure in the face of the German and Italian menace.

It was into this precarious situation that a contingent of Naafi–EFI staff, headed by Captain Tommy Shannon, arrived to build and operate canteens in Canea and at the Maleme airstrip. The project immediately ran into difficulties, as infrequent stock deliveries and erratic electricity supply, often left canteens bitterly cold and lit by flickering candlelight.

But there were some pleasant up-sides to the posting, as friendly locals, known for their hospitality, sometimes 'forced' bottles of wine, bread loaves, olives and fruit to passing Allied troops.

With the invasion of Greece by Italy and Germany in April 1941, British troops beat a hasty retreat from Athens to Crete, as EFI's Major Charles Stamp remembered: 'We were intensively dive bombed all day from Greece to Crete, but we got there and set up in an open field.'

Suddenly, Crete sat as a lone ranger in a region of dangers. Troops would meet night after night in that Naafi to share stories, whilst keeping a watchful eye on the sea. At this time, EFI began playing an operational role, including work on the hurriedly prepared defences in anticipation of an enemy attack, which eventually came on the morning of May 20th, 1941 when the buzz of German aircraft approached.

An eye-witness account, revealing how the sky was lit by German marines who became 'balls of flame' when their parachutes caught fire in the air, was given by a British soldier from Bromley, who made an epic escape from the Germans.

> A captain of the Royal Engineers ordered us back to the fort which the Aussies were holding. We got a small boat, found some very light pistols, and then went to the Naafi stores for provisions. We would have been cut off entirely had we

stayed. One German plane crashed into the water and there were no survivors. Another plane with six or seven parachutes dangling like flies on a string behind it disappeared into the sea.[68]

After weeks of fighting, Major Stamp was one of the last to leave the island after he and his party withstood a four-day stretch of attacks by German paratroopers.

He remembered that the Naafi building was once hit six times by German bombers within a period of just ten minutes. Driving for help afterwards, he briefly left his car only to return to find it destroyed by a direct hit: 'One morning we were dive bombed for two hours, and then the paratroopers dropped—around 1,500 of them. Our camp was made up of RASC, Pay Corps, Naafi, and other semi-combatant units. We set to and started to wipe up the paratroops.' Before being relieved by the Marines, EFI troops held off the Germans for four days, 'it was hand-to-hand, tree-to-tree fighting. We were also defending a strip of beach at the same time.'

After days of manning defensive positions against the advancing Germans, it was clear a retreat was essential.

Six EFI troops were killed whilst displaying supreme gallantry and despite vigorous resistance, the overwhelming weight of enemy numbers on the ground and in the air pushed the Allies southward. After nearly two-weeks of vicious fighting, the battle for Crete came to an end. The text of the official military announcement, which was broadcast to troops from Cairo, came as no surprise.

---

[68] Liverpool Evening Express, May 27th, 1941

> After twelve days of what has undoubtedly been the fiercest fighting in this war, it was decided to withdraw our forces from Crete. Although the losses we inflicted on the enemy's troops and aircraft have been enormous, it became clear that our naval and military forces could not be expected to operate indefinitely in and near Crete without more air support than could be provided from our bases in Africa. Some 15,000 of our troops have been withdrawn to Egypt, but it must be admitted that our losses have been severe.

The last evacuation of exhausted and wounded Allied soldiers wrapped-up on June 1st under almost suicidal conditions. Around 12,000 troops and thousands of Greeks remained stranded on the island and were marched in the intense heat along dirt roads into captivity. Among their numbers were two plucky EFI members, who managed to make a daring escape from a prison camp and lived for two years hidden in mountain caves, supported by locals.

In the initial confusion of the pull-out, it was not known how many soldiers had been killed, wounded or were missing, but on June 27th, 1941, a short bulletin from Cairo confirmed: 'Two officers wounded and missing, and three officers and 123 other ranks missing on Crete. This brings the total losses Naafi Expeditionary Force Institutes in the war to 320.'

***

The Mediterranean became a perilous theatre of war. It was on these high seas where an incredible tale of courage was acted out – which would change the entire course of the conflict. Even more surprising, is that the hero of the story was a sixteen-year-old Naafi canteen boy.

It was just before 05:00 on October 30th, 1942, when a British lookout on the *HMS Petard* spotted the German submarine U-559 lurking in the distance. After a long chase, the British managed to depth charge the U-boat. Shaking and rolling with each blast, the heavily damaged sub finally surfaced, and the German crew hurriedly scrambled overboard.

In their desperate dash to safety, they failed to dispose of their communications codebooks and *Enigma* machine used to transmit top-secret plans and details of military operations. When Naafi canteen boy Tommy Brown heard that the sinking submarine was to be boarded by his crewmates, he literally dived into action along with Anthony Fasson, the *Petard's* First Lieutenant, and Able Seaman Colin Grazier.

Tommy Brown

Tragically, Fasson and Grazier went down with the U-boat, but Brown emerged clutching volumes of German military cypher books, which later ended up at Bletchley Park and helped British intelligence to crack the elusive Enigma code.

Phil Shanahan is author of *The Real Enigma Heroes*: 'The importance of the incident cannot be overstated,' he says, 'as it paved the way for peace, saving countless lives.' Historians now acknowledge that the material retrieved from U-559 enabled Alan Turing and his team of scientists at Bletchley Park to crack the German four-rotor Enigma code. As a direct result of the material Tommy Brown salvaged, Allied shipping losses halved and U-boat packs began suffering losses from which they would never recover.

The story is even more remarkable when you consider that in the early 1940s, U-boats were threatening to starve Britain into surrender by sinking supply ships at twice the rate they could be built. By contrast, the number of U-boats had doubled as the Germans gained the upper hand in the war, with up to 800 thousand tonnes of Allied shipping being lost in the Atlantic on a monthly basis. Trapped in this cycle of expenditure and loss, Britain was getting ever closer to the ropes.

But, within one hour of the recovered codebooks arriving at Bletchley Park in December 1942, 15 U-boat positions were identified – meaning the British military could pinpoint German submarines and, more importantly, they knew how to avoid and destroy them.

Brown, Fasson, and Grazier's action turned the tide on the *Battle of the Atlantic*, a fight Churchill described as crucial to the outcome of the entire war.

Fasson and Grazier were posthumously awarded the *George Cross*, a decoration for bravery second only to the

Victoria Cross. But the story has a sad twist.

As the citation for Brown's *George Medal* was being drafted, it emerged that he had lied about his age in order to enlist in the Naafi. The young hero that had made one of the most vital contributions to the outcome of the war was sent packing. While alive, Brown never received his medal; he died in a house fire in 1945. His *George Cross* was awarded posthumously, making the teenage hero its youngest recipient.[69]

***

Away from the warm waters of the Mediterranean, Naafi began servicing a new *Royal Air Force* Station in Reykjavik just south of the freezing Polar region. The Navy had to navigate bitter winds and Arctic waters to ensure the new venture could operate.

The first shipment - in addition to chocolate, tinned ham and cigarettes - included thousands of books to ease the boredom of the long winter nights.

The base was operated under separate command by both the RAF and American airmen, with the Americans primarily assigned to defensive duties such as patrols and flying fighter planes, while the RAF concentrated on anti-submarine patrols with bombers. Many miles of lakes and hills were also protected by anti-aircraft batteries and observation posts, as German planes had been spotted flying over the country.

Airman L.A.C. Anthony Adams was part of the team that set up the station, which comprised mostly of Nissen huts, small ones for barrack huts, and larger but similar

---

[69] By the beginning of 1944, Naafi personnel serving in the R.A.S.C./E.F.I. or with the Naval Canteen Service had suffered over 600 casualties in killed, missing and prisoners of war.

ones for Mess halls and Naafi buildings. He noted:

> For warmth the barrack huts were lined with half-inch thick insulation wood pulp panels which we called Tentest, a coke burning tortoise stove was in the centre of each hut and we would use waste pieces of the boarding panels, easily broken, soaked in paraffin for a quick fire. The food in camp was not wonderful with porridge occasionally tainted with paraffin, Icelandic mutton alternating with *Maconochies* tinned meat and vegetable ration, by no means our favourite dish, occasionally Icelandic rhubarb and when bread ran out, as it often did, we were fed hard biscuits.[70]

Not long after Naafi opened its shutters, a bizarre incident occurred. A note was passed to the institute by the Iceland government banning the sale of English-style beer because of the country's prohibition law forbidding an alcohol content of more than two percent; the situation was only resolved when the EFI Commanding Officer personally persuaded Iceland's Prime Minister to amend the law on behalf of the Forces.[71]

During a visit in 1941, Winston Churchill paid an informal visit to the camp, where airmen cheered him during his brief stop in the Naafi hut. He also took a tour of the famous hot springs and saw one of the wonders of Iceland.

One reporter noted: 'He lingered there, greatly interested at seeing the boiling water flowing from

---

[70] Recollections of Iceland in 1941 and 1942.
http://www.ww2museum.is/l-a-c-anthony-adams-raf-in-iceland
[71] Good Morning August 29th, 1944

countless springs and in the plans to heat all Reykjavik from this volcanic heat.'

Those EFC staff worried that a posting to Iceland would be boring were left pleasantly surprised, as there was more than just the books for entertainment.

Troops jumped at the opportunity of improving their skiing, or of learning the art from the beginning. A ski club was formed, and twice week parties went on excursions in the mountains. Equipment was provided by the Naafi and RAF. The skiers included both ground staff, EFI and air crew members - some were Australians 'who had never seen snow before.'

CHAPTER 10
MARCHING WITH MONTY

Eventually, life at *Ruxley Towers* established a pattern. Every week divisional managers would be joined by the Chairman to discuss war developments. A large map in the conference room showing the vast expanse of Naafi operations was usually the starting point for these meetings. Red pins were used to indicate the location of shops and canteens in Egypt, Cyprus, Palestine, Sudan and Aden.

As the war progressed, planners were often so overwhelmed by the vast amounts of information coming in from all fronts, that it became difficult to keep track. The situation was exacerbated by the fact that freight space was hard to find and many traditional supply routes used by Naafi became too perilous to navigate. At one point, over 50-tons of supplies a day was being shipped into Naafi stores at Benghazi.

But, with increased enemy attacks on shipping, new elaborate maritime links between England and Suez in Egypt emerged. To avoid the Germans, some vessels even skirted around the Horn of Africa - covering a distance of 11,600 miles - to make a single delivery. Occasionally, cargoes were unloaded at Lagos port in Africa and then flown on to the Middle East.

Just as the logistics team started to take things in their stride, Italy declared war on the British Empire in June 1940. The situation worsened a few months later, when armed with just infantry and antiquated artillery, Mussolini's army set out to snatch Egypt. Initially – and to everyone's surprise - they made some progress, but a ferocious Allied counter-offensive kicked them back into Libya, at a cost of 200,000 of their men falling into captivity in a spectacular display of military incompetence.

The situation for the Italians worsened as they scrambled out of their strongholds at Tobruk and Benghazi in January 1941. The *Western Morning News* noted:

> The advance has been accomplished not merely by a few advanced mechanized units, but by all branches of the Army, including Naafi and the quartermasters' stores.

One British soldier remarked, 'I would like to say the Italians were enthusiastic but poorly trained. But they weren't even enthusiastic.'

With Mussolini in it up to his neck, the *Volkischer Beobachter*, the officially approved and inspired organ of the Nazi party, openly hinted that Germany would intervene to prevent an Italian defeat in Africa: 'The British really believe that Germany would look on passively Italy should grow weary? British propaganda seems to have deduced that the Third Reich intended to leave Italy in the lurch.'

The hint became reality when Hitler dispatched his newly-formed *Afrika Korps* to shore up the Italian effort in March 1941 under the command of the irrepressible Erwin Rommel. He sent three mechanized columns rumbling northward and eastward to chase the Allies along the coast road into Benghazi and then on to Barce and Derna.

Suddenly, the Allies were fighting a high-intensity conflict against a first-class enemy. The initial onslaught stunned the British, forcing them back toward Egypt - the chaos of that sudden retreat was documented by a newsman passing through Derna:

> Some three clerks of the Naafi staff wrote out lengthy documents as receipts for a purchase I made. I should have imagined they would have cut this red tape, and instead said, 'Well, the Germans are coming. Take the stuff free.' Oh no. The Germans came all right, and Naafi destroyed thousands of pounds worth of goods.

By April, the situation was vastly worse in the coastal city of Tobruk, where the British garrison had been totally cut off by the Germans, who had proven to be a formidable opponent.

EFI officer Ben White reflected glumly about German dive-bombers creating a graveyard of ships in the harbour: 'In the end, the navy brought supplies in at night anchoring just outside the harbour, unloading as much cargo as possible into Lighters and making off again before dawn.' [72]

Somehow, the encircled men kept Tobruk in Allied hands, meaning Rommel could make little headway in advancing further toward Egypt. Worse was to come: In an effort to break the impasse, Rommel unleashed hundreds of air-raids against the town, as his artillery continued to pound the garrison, forcing its defenders to exist on bare rations.

It was amid this formidable onslaught, that a Naafi truck somehow managed to race forward into the city from a

---

[72] Ben White is also mentioned in the letters of Isobel Ramsey, see *The Egypt Letters* chapter.

depot in Matruh - over 300 kilometres away - and deliver supplies, 'every man had a bottle of beer as a result of this journey – a small matter perhaps, but one which does wonders for morale.'[73]

Another morale booster came in the form of the 'Middle East cricket season' in May when soldiers in Tobruk played in their helmets before 'beating off a Hun offensive.' A press note from Naafi Cairo read: 'One thing about cricket here – rain never stopped play. Sand and mat make the pitch. The hot sand is tough on the feet but there are plenty of cricket fans.'

But the novelty of cricket balls shooting through the air, as the shelling continued didn't last long. A member of the *2nd Black Watch* reflected on the deteriorating scene, 'even the Naafi was defeated in Tobruk. Once a fortnight they could provide one razor blade per section of troops, and a twist of boiled sweets for every two or three men, cigarettes, very occasionally.'[74] Not long after, an EFI store was pinpointed by German aircraft, which resulted in five Naafi men being killed by a high explosive shell.[75]

During the onslaught, life on the garrison was like living next to a burning oil well as black smoke from the fires and bombs filled the streets and the water in the harbour blackened, thick with gasoline.

Despite the perilous reality, a *Reuter's* telegram sent on June 19th, 1942, gave no indication of how desperate things had become. It stated that as gunfire rumbled across the high escarpment, lines of men were buying tea at the Naafi canteen as others played cricket, 'but at the perimeter defences there was an atmosphere of

---

[73] Portsmouth Evening News November 28th, 1941
[74] For Love of Regiment: A History of British Infantry, Volume 2.
[75] A memorial to Naafi personnel who fell in the Middle East during the war was unveiled in Tobruk in November 1950.

watchfulness.'[76] Two days later, Tobruk and its garrison of 30,000 men fell to the Germans. James Ambrose, a South African stationed east of the city, remembered that 'every man for himself' became the order of the hour as the German army rumbled forward. One man had told him how Naafi storemen were machine-gunning stocks of beer worth £20,000. Ambrose watched men 'rushing about with cases of canned fruit, liquor, and jam. There is a mad abundance. I see men hacking tins open with bayonets, drinking the syrup and chucking the cans aside.'[77]

Malta Harbour during the war. (Authors private collection).

Whilst Rommel's success may have brought him

---

[76] Daily Mirror, June 19th, 1942

[77] Retreat to Victory: Springboks' Diary in North Africa – Gazala to El Alamein, 1942 (South Africans at War).

adulation in Berlin, new victories were scarce as it became increasingly tricky to keep his men supplied the further they advanced.

Making matters worse; the RAF flying out of Malta were sinking three in every four German supply ships sailing between Sicily and Tripoli. Once Rommel decided that Malta was to be crushed, the Luftwaffe swung into action. The tiny island was continually rocked under the thundering sound of exploding bombs and anti-aircraft defences - the sheer intensity of the raids made it the most bombed place on earth.

Norman Reginald Gill, an RAMC radiographer described his experience: 'Most shops were closed because they had been bombed or because they had nothing to sell. There was not a lot of point in going into Valletta because there was nothing to buy.'

Surprisingly, Naafi on the island increased the number of canteens and shops from 17 in 1939, to 80 by 1942. 'Hardly a day went by without four or five canteens being damaged,' Brigadier W.N. Hamilton, the Naafi supervisor in Valetta later recorded. Incredibly, only two staff members were killed during the siege.

As the Germans attacked the dockyards, aerodromes and residential districts, the words *'Player's Please'* – the name of a famous cigarette brand - beamed across the British Army communication radios and during prolonged raids: *'More Player's Please.'* It was later revealed that the phrase was used in naval orders as a secret code for ordering and extending the island's protective smoke screens. (*Player's* were exceptionally strong and emitted huge puffs of smoke.)

When the raids were over, canteen staff tended the wounded, swept up the debris and opened up again. Regardless of the terrific intensity of the barrage, an

ENSA concert party continued to play to the troops without a break for nearly three years. The *Whizz Bangs* —comprising four men and four women—were the only wartime concert party on the island. Each night, as the bombs fell, units of the garrison would settle down to enjoy a twenty-six-item programme.

In spite of the vicious onslaught, Malta was not subdued and Major J. C. Burke, Naafi's commander on the island, wrote after the war that his greatest moment was watching Italian Fleet sail to Valetta to surrender in September 1943. 'The islanders,' he said, 'did not cheer. They simply stared open-mouthed, at the awe-inspiring sight.'

***

Meanwhile, the seesaw tussle between the *Eighth Army* and *Afrika Korps* continued amidst the vast flat wilderness of the Western Desert. Under Bernard Montgomery, who was appointed desert commander in 1942, the British Army became a vastly more effective force than it had been.

Battles also continued at sea off the Libyan coast, with three Naafi workers being killed when the destroyer *Sikh* was sunk by shore batteries near Tobruk, and the minesweeper *Leda* was blasted apart by U-435 on September 20th, 1942.

By October that year, things were very different, as Allied forces inflicted a series of decisive victories over the Germans, reaching a climax at the *Second Battle of El Alamein* when Rommel's men fell into a headlong retreat across the desert and eventual surrender in May 1943. The speed with which Naafi carried supplies to the *Eighth Army* during its pursuit of Rommel's forces was indicated in report from their Middle East headquarters, which stated: 'So rapidly was the Naafi on the scene after the Allies had driven the Germans from El Salloum (East of Tobruk), that remnants of the retreating Axis forces were coming into the Naafi stores and giving themselves up.'

A month after the defeat, Lieutenant D. Fenley, an officer with the South Staffordshire Regiment, passed through the Alamein positions observing, 'an endless trail of wrecked tanks, vehicles, abandoned shells, and graves of both sides.' He added:

> On, on, we went to Tobruk, where we camped about five miles from the sea and town. It was an uninteresting camp, though we were having a day's rest. The amount of salvaged German stuff was amazing.[78]

When the *Eighth Army* marched into the Libyan capital Tripoli, Naafi established it's only brewing enterprise in the Middle East, from where thousands of crates of beer were transported along several hundred miles of desert road in lorry convoys to Benghazi and Tobruk.

Empty bottles were the main problem, collecting them and returning them for refilling proved a gargantuan task. Supply trucks stopped off at new Naafi 'roadhouses' (hastily thrown together pubs) which sprung up along dusty desert roads and were given names like *The Ship Inn* and *Noah's Ark*. With supply-routes still patchy, these new establishments were furnished using some ingenious improvisation by Naafi. In one district, over 50 tons of wooden railway sleepers were purchased and crafted into tables, chairs, counters and shelves. Glasses were

---

[78] Lichfield Mercury, July 30th, 1943

produced by cutting the necks off beer bottles and smoothing the rims, whilst plates and cups were made by melting down broken bottles.

In a blow to Herman Goring's vanity, news of a German *Heinkel* transport plane being used by the RAF as a 'flying brewer's dray' was broadcast on the *BBC Home Service*. The plane had been captured intact and went on to fly thousands of pints of beer to settle the dust in North Africa.

For many of the men enjoying a refreshing beer, entertainment was provided by an unknown young comedian called Tommy Cooper, who had joined Montgomery's army in Egypt, and then became a member of a Naafi entertainment party. He developed an act around his magic tricks mixed with comedy.

His trademark red fez was introduced to his routine by chance during a Naafi concert in Cairo, after the helmet he planned on wearing vanished. Instead, he borrowed the waiter's hat – and a legend was born.

Once the desert campaign was over Monty left for London. For many who knew him, Montgomery was an enigma. After the war, he remarked that 'some think that morale is best sustained when the British soldier is surrounded by Naafi clubs, canteens, and so on. I disagree. My experience with soldiers is that they are at their best when they are asked to face up to hard conditions.'[79] This view didn't stop him sending a note to Naafi in December 1943, requesting stores for his 'personal Mess' to brighten his Christmas on the battlefront, or stocking up with perfume during a fleeting visit to Berlin a few years later. [80]

---

[79] The Memoirs of Field Marshal Montgomery by Bernard Law Montgomery of Alamein
[80] Naafi Up! AQ & DJ Publications.

Another curious fact about the Middle East theatre emerged after the war, when it was revealed Winston Churchill had kept his own 'cigar Mess' in Egypt.

The stash was one of the closely guarded secrets of the war and concerned of a stock of Havana cigars held in a cool cellar beneath Naafi's main shop in Cairo and specially reserved for the Prime Minister for when he visited the region.

It transpired that even senior officers on G.H.Q. staff who called regularly at the shop knew nothing of the secret stock. After the war, a *Reuter's* correspondent revealed that when Churchill met Generalissimo Chiang Kai-Shek, and later at the Fayoum, where he visited King Ibn Suad of Saudi Arabia, his cigars were supplied direct from the Cairo shop.

Those on Naafi staff who knew their destination were sworn to secrecy.

***

Another area where the British felt the full force of their enemies was in Asia. After their stunning attack on Pearl Harbour on December 8th, 1941, Japan turned their eyes toward the Philippines, Burma, Thailand, the Dutch East Indies, Malaya, and Singapore.

Hong Kong was the first British possession to fall in December 1941, where a Naafi contingent remained supporting the troops, as locally employed staff signed-up with the *Hong Kong Defence Force*.

Captain D.W Joyce, the assistant to the district manager, recounted that from the outset the onslaught was a nightmare, especially when the territory fell after 18-days of fighting. 'We were ordered to clear up battle areas, sorting out Jap dead, whose bodies were afterwards ceremoniously burnt. The British dead were just rolled down the hillside,' he recalled. 'In the places we had to leave our wounded -they had been bayoneted to death - and those who were less hurt had been tied to trees and used for bayonet practice.'

In a gesture of spite, the Japanese gave Joyce the additional harrowing task of cutting bodies down from the trees, many of whom had been his personal friends. He was then marched into a prisoner of war camp.

Japan marched on to chalk-up an extraordinary series of victories. On January 2nd, 1942, they took Manila, followed by an attack on the Dutch East Indies on January 11th. The next day Kuala Lumpur fell and 72-hours later, Burma was subjected to the might of the Japanese onslaught.

Then, Malaya was gradually occupied at the cost of 50,000 Allied Prisoners of War. As the Japanese pushed forward, ninety canteens were abandoned as staff made a beeline for Singapore, where district manager Arthur Perry, had been enjoying a peaceful life since arriving with his bride in 1940.

He had joined the institute as an enthusiastic 21-year-old in 1934 and chalked up service in the UK, Hong Kong and Malta.

Suddenly, Perry was in the thick of it, as Singapore's strategic importance and value as a supplier of rubber and tin was on the ropes. English, Scottish, Australian, Indian and Chinese troops put up a brave battle against the invaders amid the mangrove swamps and plantations. But this brave last-ditch effort was not enough, as the Japanese fighting prowess had been underestimated.

As the enemy approached, Arthur went into his EFI role as Captain ACT Perry RAOC/EFI No: 205360 and was tasked with burying the bodies of those killed by shells which were smashing down across the city. The bodies were placed in graves near the Naafi headquarters on Anson Road, once that task had been completed; Perry smashed thousands of bottles of wines and spirits at the Naafi warehouse.

Even at the last moment, many expatriates played a guessing game as to whether Japan could still win, but such conversations ended abruptly when the garrison surrendered.

'Just before the fall of Singapore in February 1942, saw my mother shipped off to Australia on one of the last ships to escape from Singapore, pregnant with my sister, armed only with a suitcase of clothes and her *Singer* sewing machine and a teddy bear for the unborn child,' Arthur Perry's son John later recalled. Other Naafi wives – ten in all - manged to board vessels to Durban and UK.

The capture of Singapore was one of the great blows to Allied morale and the largest surrender of British-led military personnel in history, as 80,000 British, Indian and Australian troops were marched into captivity.

Without reinforcements of troops, planes, food and munitions, Singapore was always destined to be captured by the Japanese or forced to surrender.

When it fell, it represented a disaster of the first magnitude to the British position in the Pacific. The German propaganda apparatus in Berlin predicted that Gibraltar 'the last of the pillars of the British Empire' would soon be lost. A Nazi radio commentary stated that: 'The new Spain will not forever tolerate seeing it in British hands.' Such gloomy reports, which were repeated ad nauseam, were buttered up after Rangoon fell in March when the British withdrew from Burma.

For Churchill, it represented the worst disaster and largest capitulation in British history. Arthur Perry was sent to the *Changi Prison* complex, initially in one of the external camp bungalows, but later within the prison itself, before being transferred to *No 2 POW Camp* in Thailand, where he was forced to work on the infamous Burma Railway - also known as the *Death Railway*.

'My mother got official notification that he had been taken as a POW from the War Office in December 1942. The family received just three Japanese communication postcards from Arthur during his period of internment as a POW,' John recalled. His father eventually spent three-and-a-half years in captivity.

***

The losses in Asia came after Naafi recorded a few turbulent few years, plagued by other losses in southern Europe and Africa. The institute reported a turnover of £72million for the second war year, converting a deficiency of £393,000 for the first year to a surplus of £1.5million.

Losses in respect of evacuations from Greece and Crete amounted to £119,610. The withdrawal in the Western Desert cost £250,000 and in Malaya losses were estimated at over £200,000. Despite that, Naafi was able to return of a record £4.3million to the services in cash and amenities.

By the end of 1942, staff numbered over 72,000, and the number of establishments in the UK stood at 5,800 and there were 620 institutes and 100 warehouses and bulk issue stores overseas.

With the war in the desert over, all eyes turned to Italy, where a combined Allied invasion of Sicily began on July 10th, 1943, with both amphibious and airborne landings.

Naafi canteen stores touched-down just eighty hours

behind the first assault parties, with the BBC stating on July 16th that: 'News was received in London yesterday that Naafi goods and personnel have been landed on the beaches of Sicily.'

By any standards this was remarkable. Naafi men were shadowing the assault troops at Anzio on Italy's west coast by March 1944, as chairman Lancelot Royle visited the beachhead to see how his staff worked under the enemy's nose.

The EFI contingent was lead by 32-year-old Lieutenant 'Jock' Walker, along with twelve men, all veterans of North Africa. They managed to erect a bulk issue store and shop just days after the first landings, a feat that gained a huge amount of praise.

Finally, after weeks of intense fighting, the Anzio campaign reached a stalemate. Yet, when long-awaited reinforcements arrived in May, the Allies broke out and ultimately marched victoriously into Rome, where Naafi took over a former seven-storey department store, which they named the *Alexander Club*.

They bestrew it with elaborate wall mouldings, frescoes, arches and chandeliers. It was not surprising then when the club became one of the biggest draws in Rome, with its white-jacketed waiters darting around the huge restaurant, a trendy ice cream palace on the top floor serving traditional ices, and a cinema, which ran a non-stop programme of the latest films.

The Alexander Club offered customers packets of 16 postcards displaying the restaurants, bars and gift shop.

The *Alexander Club* was a popular haunt for many visiting stars on ENSA tours. On one occasion, Gracie Fields sang her hit song 'Sally' whilst wiggling in glittery high-heeled stilettos as a thousand Tommies cheered with delight; she also thrilled local waitresses by reeling-off a few songs in Italian.

In the space of one year, Naafi had moved from the dirty, dusty, un-swept canteens of the western desert to Roman-style luxury. The *Alexander* set the mould for the Naafi Club era to come.

At the same time, the biggest Naafi canteen in the world at the *Royal Palace Naples* opened its doors. A visiting reporter said it took over an hour walk around and catered for 10,000 people every day, with seating for 7,000.

CHAPTER 11
YANKS AHOY!

When the first GIs landed in Britain in 1942, they were greeted with both relief and curiosity. These 'willing, eager and ready' troops first stopped in Northern Ireland where a Naafi reception party handed out cups of tea. The institute had prepared for this moment, by issuing a special booklet of advice to their girls on familiarizing them with American history, culture, eating habits and even the slang.

Naafi said they hoped the advice would promote a better understanding of America and Americans and stop the little quarrels between Naafi girls and American soldiers which could develop.

When you meet the Americans advised that dishes such as hot dogs (described as 'fried sausages in split rolls') and hamburgers, (savoury rissoles between slices of bread) were particular favourites with GIs. [81] Furthermore, it stated that a 'surprisingly large' number of Americans were teetotal, which in native speak was referred to as being 'up the pole'. [82]

Given that the 1.5 million US servicemen in Britain would probably encounter difficulties with the local bureaucracy, 'purchase tax' and the use of ration

---

[81] *When you meet the Americans*, Naafi internal publication. 1942.

[82] Harry Miller, the Naafi historian, noted that some American units were actually willing to barter jeeps for scotch, because the prohibition back in the states left them frequently short of spirits.

'coupons' were to be fully explained.

There was sage advice for that first encounter when an American limbered up to the counter and uttered: 'Howdy baby.'

The first American GI's arrive in Ulster are greeted by Naafi girls.

'You probably think he is being impudent,' the pamphlet explained. 'By the time several dozen men have said it, you'll have come to the conclusion that all Americans are 'fresh'.' It was pointed out that the saying was 'merely a conversational opening' just as the British say 'lovely day isn't it?'

It was also asserted that most Americans thought the British were standoffish: 'If you snub them, it will merely confirm that impression.'

> Under that breezy manner, most of them are a little shy and they will show their appreciation of your kindness if you take them for what they are - pleasant, young American boys. Try not to appear shocked at some of their expressions, some of

this may sound remarkably like swearing to you, but it is, in fact, that they are everyday words in use in America.

Furthermore, the pamphlet 'translated' American to English; for example, definitions were given for the meaning of cookies, candy, highball and French fries. 'If they ask for their change in 'bills', they mean notes.'

A few hints for canteen staff fed-up by Americans of the 'gabby' variety were also provided:

> You make think that they are inclined to make too much of the skyscrapers of New York, the lights of Manhattan, the extent of the prairies or Niagara. If you find yourself to be irritated by their talk, it means you cannot find things to equal them in Britain. True, we have not got a Woolworths Building, but then again, America has not got a thousand-year-old Tower of London.

The booklet concludes: 'Every time to lose your temper with an American, or refuse to understand his point of view, you are fighting Hitler's battles for him. Don't help Hitler.'

A couple of final tips are worth mentioning. Girls were encouraged to be 'a little friendlier' than they normally would, and if possible, to avoid talking about 'Chicago gangsters as if they represented 90 per cent of the population.'

In a similar vein, the *United States War Department* published a small booklet of tips offering *Instructions for American Servicemen*. Pointers included:

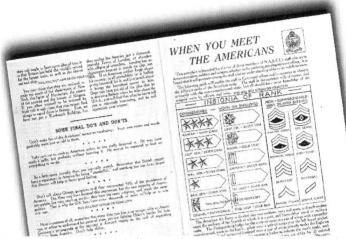

The pamphlet 'translated' American to English; for example, definitions were given for the meaning of cookies, candy, highball and French fries.

'When you see a girl in khaki or air-force blue with a bit of ribbon on her tunic – remember she didn't get it for knitting more socks than anyone else in Ipswich.' Also: 'If you are invited to eat with a family don't eat too much. Otherwise, you may eat up their weekly rations,' and: 'Don't make fun of British speech or accents. You sound just as funny to them but they will be too polite to show it.'

Other nuggets of advice urged GI's to 'NEVER criticize the King or Queen,' and 'The British don't know how to make a good cup of coffee. You don't know how to make a good cup of tea. It's an even swap.'

Whilst many Americans frequented Naafi canteens, most of the bigger US garrisons had their own *Post Exchanges*, known as the PX operated by the army on a non-profit basis. PX also ran hairdressers, shoe shops, photo booths and restaurants, whilst their stores stocked everything from soap and cigarettes, to food and clothing to gift articles. British soldiers accustomed to austerity at home and in the Army, were staggered by the profusion of goods in PX stores. The Brits lucky enough to have experienced dining at an American *Red Cross Club* - remarked the contrast with Naafi: 'Now I can understand why we are not allowed in—except with an American,' wrote one soldier, who had salty words for the institute. He said: 'Being strictly civilian, the American canteens treated customers differently, whereas 'our Naafi's are pervaded by the military spirit.' He added:

> There was a queue there, too. But it moved much more quickly than ours. Why? There is only a counter between the girls who served and the kitchen. The kitchen staff put the filled plates on the counter— and the girls who serve just turn round pick them up. And another fact is that the Naafi executive consists of retired Generals, Air Marshals, and Admirals. I, at any rate, have never stood in a Naafi queue with any of them.

An old army gag told the story of a soldier in a canteen queue, who, feeling thoroughly 'browned-off,' suddenly left the line announcing that he was going to shoot the sergeant-major. A few minutes later he returned. Asked if he had shot the sergeant-major, he gloomily shook his head. 'No,' he said. 'There was a queue for that too.'
Such negative attitudes about the Naafi became common. Reports of 'rude service' was picked up by the *Daily Mirror*, which had received 'some spirited repudiations' that Naafi staff might be 'more polite, friendly, and helpful' to the men who used the canteens. However, an editorial concluded:

We are informed, in fact, that the boot is on the other foot. The men, it is alleged, are often rude, unreasonable, and domineering. Waitresses say that their hours are long and their pay small. If part of those huge profits could be spent on improving the lot of the girls, and part on lowering the prices for Tommy, a mutual feeling of goodwill might develop.

CHAPTER 12
SECOND FRONT

PLANS for liberating Europe with a naval, air and land assault on Nazi-occupied France had tentatively been underway since 1941. When it finally happened on June 6th, 1944, Allied troops landed along a 50-mile stretch of Normandy coastline in the first stage of an audacious bid to free Europe from Hitler.[83]

Naafi plans for its part in the *Second Front* were thrashed out in a makeshift office at St. Paul's School in London by Brigadier W.H Hamilton and future chairman Major William Beale, both Africa campaign veterans.[84]

They said experiences gained in North Africa, Sicily, and Southern Italy would be utilized and there would be no repeat of Dunkirk. An advanced guard of R.A.S.C men attached to Naafi would follow the first assault troops and set up bulk issue stores near the front line. Units could then draw stores, which were distributed to individual soldiers.'[85] Naafi transports would move at the command of military authorities and a fleet of mobile canteens was placed in storage awaiting orders.

The idea was, that as the beachhead at Normandy expanded with fighting moving further inland, Naafi would open base canteens, clubs, and restaurants. At this stage, female staff members were to appear on the scene.

---

[83] D-Day was originally set for June 5 but had to be postponed for 24 hours because of bad weather.

[84] On June 6th, 1944, that the Allies opened 'a second front' in Europe with the invasion of Normandy.

[85] Yorkshire Post and Leeds Mercury, June 8th, 1944

But, before any such plans could be executed, huge manpower challenges needed addressing. A series of recruitment adverts in ran in newspapers during the first few months of 1944. One campaign announced:

> ...to keep faith with the forces, Naafi needs a steady flow of recruits—men and women in paid employment as cooks, counter assistants, and general assistants. The need for Naafi is greater than ever—join today.

Hundreds of male reservists signed on, along with 1,600 female volunteers. In March 1944, appeals were posted asking for volunteers to 'go under canvas' for six-weeks to serve thousands of troops herded together at docks and at camps on the southern coast of England.

Nora Neale was 'barbed-wired in' at *Camp S6* near Brentwood: 'It was hard work and we couldn't go out of the camp. No letters went out either.'

Further south, Ida Owens was at Southampton Water: 'We slept under canvas, although for three days and three nights we hardly slept at all, snatching an hour's sleep when we could. Up and down the lines of soldiers we went, dispensing hot drinks, snacks and cigarettes and baking the famous rock buns in the field kitchen. The soldiers were in good spirits, but mostly very tensed up, they seemed so very young.'[86]

Another Naafi girl was sent to the Wanstead Flats in Epping Forest which was being used as a marshalling area for D-Day troops. 'It was all so quiet. We were told we could be shot if we walked within 14-feet of the fence. We were there from April 1944. We slept in tents and had

---

[86] BBC, WW2 People's War. Article ID: A4269891, 25 June 2005

to wash in a long communal trough, with small bowls of cold water. We did have a hip bath in a small tent.'[87]

Nora Neale would never forget watching the troops finally march-off: 'Highland divisions went to the sound of the bagpipes, quite moving really, as we wondered how many would survive.'

The men set off with tiny cardboard boxes known as 'Naafi pack' kits – stuffed with cigarettes, chocolates, toothpaste, razor blades, soap, meat extract cubes, pencils, note paper, milk powder, and chewing gum. The sustaining powers of chocolate were by this point 'officially recognized' and four-fifths of the total output from the Bournville factory was being purchased by Government priorities like Naafi.

Operation Overlord was finally launched on June 6th, 1944, when 156,000 troops under the command of General Bernard Montgomery, supported by 8,000 ships and 13,000 airplanes headed for France.

On the eve of battle, General Eisenhower told Allied forces: 'You are about to embark upon a great crusade, toward which we have striven these many months. The eyes of the world are upon you.'

The day of the invasion had been repeatedly postponed because of blustery weather. When it happened, the armada of destroyers, minesweepers, landing craft, and merchant ships made-up the largest maritime force ever assembled.

In the skies above, the busy drone of RAF planes could be heard heading to France to 'soften up' the Germans. Salvo after salvo – the planes swooped overhead, dropping bombs and firing at machine-gun nests in the famed *Atlantic Wall*.

---

[87] BBC, WW2 People's War. Article ID: A4416013

Huge allied losses were recorded, with over 10,000 men killed in those first days. The ensuing *Battle of Normandy* resulted in Allied casualties of more than 190,000 and reduced nearly 610 towns and villages to rubble, but the Allies ultimately prevailed. At the end of the first day, along with more than 150,000 men, 22,000 jeeps, cars, and tanks had been landed.

It took seventeen-days after the first landings before a Naafi reconnaissance party surveyed the French coast, to seek out a suitable location for a storage depot. Only in early July did five mobile canteens begin service, after a depot in Sully opened to receive over 1,000 tons of goods a week.[88]

Later that same month, Naafi publicity claimed their plans were falling into place perfectly, and their efforts in Normandy were to 'the complete satisfaction of the Military Command.' On June 29th, every national and provincial newspaper in Britain ran Naafi-sponsored high-falutin prose about 'marching close upon the heels of Britain's invasion army, pledging to serve the fighting men, whenever they pause for rest and refreshment.'

> Invasion is no new experience for Naafi. Crete ... Greece ... North Africa ... Sicily ... Salerno . . . Anzio — in all these hazardous landings, Naafi men and supplies 'shadowed' the assault troops.
> Yet these campaigns are dwarfed beside the immense challenge and high adventure of D-Day. To Naafi, the opening of the *Second Front* means the crucial test of many months of careful

---

[88] Soon after, nearly half a million cigarettes, 30 million bottles of beer and 9,500 tons of assorted goods were landed, along with 800 canteen workers.

planning and well-kept secrets. It means movement orders for thousands of tons of canteen goods, cunningly dispersed yet easily assembled; it means 'action stations' for thousands of canteen men and girls trained and held in readiness for the big show. It means the *Naval Canteen Service* operating at full capacity. It means 'stand to' for a fleet of mobile canteens, for *Second Front* concert parties, and for all those follow-up Naafi services waiting their turn in the invasion queue. It means above all, the greatest opportunity for service ever presented to a canteen organisation, and Naafi accepts it with sober confidence. Difficulties and obstacles will abound, but they will be overcome so that at the end it may be said with truth that from 'D-Day' to 'V-Day,' from the landing beaches to the ruins of Berlin, Naafi pressed forward, dedicated to the service of Britain's fighting forces.

As each day passed, journalist Richard McMillan became increasingly irritated by the adverts: 'I wish we could get some advertisements about Naafi written by the boys out there,' he wrote. 'I have heard the sad tale from soldiers on many fronts, and it is always the same. Where does the money go? Where is the beer? Why don't the cigarettes come along in time?' McMillan had been tipped-off that some theatres were undersupplied – and in some cases not even reachable.

'What's happened to Naafi?' they ask. They have been asking that since D-Day when they stormed across the beachheads. Of course, they did not expect to see the Naafi canteens right away. The invasion machinery had to go in first. But they hoped that, after a few days at least, some cigarettes might come along. After all, Naafi has always boasted in paid-for advertisements about what it did for the troops. But the boys on the beachheads waited—and waited, without their fags. And beer!

But wherever the fighting' is hottest, such as on the beaches, you will find Naafi absent, I know what the answer is. The invariable reply to such criticisms is that the 'exigencies of the operations' prevent the landing of Naafi stores until a later date. But why do the exigencies of the situation prevent such a comparatively easy operation. If Naafi had the proper push and drive and authority - which one would expect from an organisation which has amassed millions in trade, with the soldiers—it should be able to insist that it be allowed to take risks to try and land comforts.[89]

Engineer Richard 'Dicker' Williams was lucky enough to see a mobile canteen on July 21st. 'We had our first visit from the old Naafi van yesterday. I got some chewing gum, razor blades etc. I get a bar of choc and about a dozen boiled sweets every day so there's no shortage in this respect.'[90] Soon, the push forward had gathered an unstoppable momentum, but the Naafi vans traveled slowly, with frequent halts and as troops fanned-out, it

---

[89] A kick in the pants for NAAFI – from the boys. Daily Mirror, July 11th, 1944.

[90] Letter written by Richard 'Dicker' Williams - an army mechanic - to his sweetheart. July 21st, 1944.

became a struggle to cope.

'What I think of the Naafi is better not printed,' a furious WREN wrote to the *Daily Mirror*. 'I have received a letter from my husband in Normandy asking me to send him envelopes, soap, toothpaste, etc., because he cannot buy any of them, as 'things are not yet highly organized.' The response from the *Daily Mirror* was acidic, to say the least:

> Perhaps the various Service officers liaisoned in *Ruxley Towers*, the Naafi headquarters, will spare a few moments from that excellent and well-stocked bar of theirs to look into this. There are enough of them, goodness knows. The last time we were there the place looked like a Battalion headquarters. [91]

As complaints persisted, Naafi rejected accusations of being careless planners – but it was a very public humiliation. By the middle of August, they announced that 675 million cigarettes, 96,0001b of tobacco and three-million boxes of matches, in addition to three-million tablets of soap, nine-million razor blades, and the equivalent 101 million bars of chocolate had been shipped to Normandy. Claude Luke, who was by then the Naafi public relations officer, observed:

> The mobile canteens in the advanced areas had an outstandingly successful staff. Soldiers were often amazed to see a thin-skinned vehicle so far

---

[91] *Daily Mirror* August 1, 1944.

forward. The headache of the commanding officer was always lest they go too far forward. Naafi has suffered casualties among the staff working in the advanced areas, and one of our mobile canteens has even been bringing in prisoners. The mobile canteen men, who are specially trained in the use of small arms, carry a Sten gun with them.

Luke also confirmed that millions of cigarettes destined for the British Liberation Army had been stolen since D-Day, and large quantities had found their way to the Continent, to be sold at extortionate prices.

Ex-Scotland Yard officers were attached to Naafi's own C.I.D. branch and sent to France and Belgium and engaged on a point-to-point check-up of consignments.

Military police with trained watchdogs also guarded bulk issue stores. 'We are also paying special attention our home service troops' supplies,' Luke said. 'In one case we lost several million cigarettes when two black market lorries drove up to one of our dumps and loaded up with the cigarettes, which were afterwards offered for sale in the London area.'

***

ENSA concert parties crossed the Channel to entertain the troops in early July, using twelve mobile columns consisting of four parties carrying a dozen vehicles— including travelling coaches, sleeping coaches, lorries that could be swiftly converted into stages and mobile workshops. Among the first to land in France were George Formby, Leslie Henson, Solomon, the pianist, and Gertrude Lawrence.

By the end of August, sixty static-canteens and 100 mobile units had opened in France. Sports goods were sent as a free gift to soldiers, and the thousands of men who had been in the heavy fighting were seen bathing wearing Naafi swim shorts. But, the task of delivering comforts to the fighting man was, in fact, not much better by October. Richard 'Dicker' Williams found it hard to fathom-out what was happening.

> The Naafi van has just turned up – for the first time since Normandy and even now, they've got no tobacco. Makes me mad to think of it, especially when people in England imagine that the fighting soldier gets everything he needs. We're always hearing talk of 'Officer Shops' but in four months over here, I haven't been able to buy a collar stud even!

In November, Sir Lancelot C. Royle gave a hearty send-off to the first civilian Naafi personnel heading-off to serve in Western Europe. The new canteen and office staff were employed in the rear establishments in France, as the forward Naafi canteens continued to be staffed by the Expeditionary Force Institutes.

Soon after, Royle announced impressive profits of £3.7million for the fourth year of the war. He said £1.8million was handed over for Naafi-ENSA shows; £73,447 was spent on sports goods, newspapers and canteens, £1.7million given to the Service welfare and benevolent funds, leaving £11,917 in the till.

Naafi civilian staff are to operate in Western Europe. A newspaper advert from November, 1944.

CHAPTER 13
INTO EUROPE

ON every street they liberated, the Allies were cheered on by pensioners, kids, priests, the poor, policemen and enthusiastic young girls throwing flowers and blowing kisses.

The people had never seen anything like this, as the tide in Europe finally turned. In the space of a little less than a year, the British and their Allies drove the German Army back from the beaches of Normandy, across France, through the Low Countries and into the brick and slate wastelands of Germany.

After the ropey start following D-Day, Naafi managed to pull its act together, but there remained many practical problems to overcome, such as how would troops on active service pay for their purchases? British soldiers took with them many things – kit, weapons, rations and water, but seldom money. They would hardly be dashing into occupied France with a pocketful of shillings. To solve the problem, millions of brown octagonal plastic half-franc tokens were manufactured to prevent a shortage of small change in Naafi canteens. Actually, the idea was not new, beer tokens, supper coupons, tea-chits, dividend stamps and even tickets for 'one tot of gin' had been used in some theatres where currency tokens replaced Lire, Mils, St James Kavlier, Shillings and Egyptian pounds.

On Saturday August 26th, 1944, Paris was liberated when the Second French Armoured Division reached the city centre. Children were hitched-up by soldiers onto their great tanks; as the liberators were showered with embraces and kisses. One correspondent noted:

> It was wonderful to see the Seine flowing under its undamaged bridges, in this lovely August sunshine. Wonderful too was the sight of thousands of cyclists in the broad avenue of the Champs Elysees. A gay whirl of colour flowing in two great streams up and down the boulevard, and round the Arc de Triomphe, from which a huge French tricolour billowed in the breeze.

A resplendent Naafi officers' club at the Rothschild mansion in the Rue du Foubourg, near the British Embassy, held nightly dances where patrons could dine for three shillings and use the bar, garden and games room.

The institute was displaying a remarkable talent for converting occupied properties into plush clubs. The sight of British soldiers, travel-stained and weary, climbing out of Army trucks on boulevards in Paris was common during late 1944. Most of them were heading for the *British Other Ranks' Leave Club* at the Ambassadors Hotel, the first hostel to be opened by the W.V.S. under the auspices of the Naafi and EFI.

With the liberation of France, victory was finally in sight and by September, Allied troops had made a triumphal entry into Brussels in tanks, trucks and armoured cars. 'Never have troop carriers had so many lovely girls aboard; never have jeeps been so gracefully draped in flowers,' American correspondent Austin Hatton observed. 'The frenzy that possesses these people must be seen to be believed.'

Accordingly, the Allied headquarters moved to the

Belgian capital, where venues like the *Blighty Café*, *YWCA*, and the *21-Club* sprang up to serve the forces. The latter, an enormous dance venue, was designed by tycoon Billy Butlin, who had been idle since the demise of the tourist trade in 1939.[92] For his Brussels project, Butlin sketched plans—loosely based on his Skegness holiday camp ballroom—which included a vast dance floor, orchestra stage, bar, restrooms, and lobby area. With a capacity of 3,000, it was an instant hit; most nights after 9pm all roads led there, as the orchestra belted out popular tunes into the early hours.

The cobbled streets of Brussels could be lively after midnight, especially as junior ranks had spruced themselves up at the *Montgomery Club*—the de-facto focal point of social life. Before hitting the town, troops often strengthened their Naafi beer by adding a few drops of Calvados, a very potent local apple brandy.

Named after the Field Marshall, the *Montgomery Club* was so plush that Naafi produced glossy picture postcards of it for soldiers to send home.[93] The club was located at the *Palais d'Egmont* in the city centre near the Palace of Justice. The distinctive, steel crest of the Naafi, anchored in front of the main gates, welcomed thousands of war-weary troops. Sadly, Naafi does not appear in the building's 'official history,' which is posted on an enamel tourist sign on the main gate. But today, the exterior and gardens do though remain largely unchanged since the 1940s. Nowadays, the sumptuous space plays host to a diverse roster of government events and retains much of

---

[92] In 1939, Billy Butlin rented out his holiday camps "for the duration" to the War Office, which converted them into barracks for both the army and navy.

[93] A prized photo in the Naafi press armoury shows a smiling Montgomery signing the visitors' book.

its old-world charm, as well as the labyrinth of dimly lit rooms. The entrance hall is grandly decorated in marble and gilt - crowned by a chandelier. A marble staircase dividing into two sweeps up to the floors above.

In 1944, on the right-hand side would have stood the Naafi shop; in the centre a box for suggestions; and on the left an information desk with several receptionists, all speaking English and waiting to arrange anything from a tour of Brussels to a Russian lesson. One popular attraction, somewhat of a busman's holiday, was tours of the battlefields at Waterloo, where the Duke of Wellington defeated Napoleon.

The club was a popular haunt for war-correspondents, looking for gossip and tittle-tattle from the front. One reporter, Willie Stewart, claimed that the German army had used the palace to plan an occupation of the United Kingdom: 'To the Germans,' he wrote, 'it was the building where they installed printing presses for the large-scale maps in which every city and big town, every piece of coastline and every military objective in Britain was marked out in amazing detail.' The Germans did indeed use the building, but primarily as a social venue. A statue of Peter Pan in the gardens had been utilized as a target for revolver practice, where trigger-happy German officers left bullet holes through its heart, right arm, and thigh.

Scottish correspondent Lucy Moorehead was suitably impressed on her visit to the club, reporting that hot meals were served all day and soldiers could take a bath and get a haircut.[94] She was thrilled to see that servicemen could write letters, read the papers, dance, have their photograph taken, or even send flowers home:

---

[94] "Gaiety, Cleanliness and Comfort" Falkirk Herald April 18th, 1945

'There is nothing even remotely smacking of the institution about it,' she gushed. Even notices and directions went out of their way to be polite: *'Would you mind leaving your coat in the cloakroom,'* for instance. Or *'kindly try and keep this door shut.'*

There was a writing room with desks and painted flower shades on the lamps. Each desk had ink, pens, and notepaper, including special airmail letter forms. In the 'news corridor' papers from all over England, Scotland, and Canada were set out on tables or pegged to hooks.

> In the ladies' hairdressing section a dozen ATS and WAAFs were having their hair done. I looked at the price list; two shillings for a shampoo and set; one shilling for a manicure; 12s 6d for a permanent wave. In the next room two ATS corporals were pressing their uniforms and other girls were mending their clothes or making things on the sewing machines provided. All this free.

With such coverage, Naafi's self-esteem glowed amid the praise. Now, it was time to think about the next stop... Germany.

CHAPTER 14
LETTERS FROM EGYPT

BEFORE joining Bernard Montgomery on the march to Berlin - we first turn the clock back to 1939 and meet Isobel Ramsey, a Naafi employee in Egypt. She started writing weekly letters home to her father in Scotland - every one is filled remarkable details. All human life is there.[95] Her correspondence began when she left her Naafi job in London for a supervisor post in Cairo.[96] Between embarking on the *SS Stratheden* bound for Port Said on April 6th 1939, and her return six-years later, Isobel painted a tantalising portrait of everyday life working for Naafi in wartime Egypt.

Just eight-months before Isobel boarded the *SS Stratheden*, Eric Arthur Blair, more commonly known as George Orwell, bid farewell to England on the very same vessel. Long journeys could be an ordeal. According to his wife Eileen, he 'walked around the ship with a seraphic smile, watching people being sick and insisted on

---

[95] Isobel Ramsey correspondence relating to her time in Egypt as archived in the Glasgow Women's Library. Her duties included overseeing catering events and parties. Occasionally, she supervised local Naafi canteens.

[96] From Cairo, in addition to running canteens, clubs, and a catering division, the institute ensured the smooth operation of 900-plus vehicles deployed along the roads and tracks of the Sudan, Eritrea, East Africa, Aden, Palestine, the Lebanon, Syria, Transjordan, Iraq, Iran, Cyprus, and Ceylon. Naafi orders from Cairo directed more than 450 enlisted drivers, including seven women. Their heavy trucks carried essential supplies thousands of miles each week. Mobile canteens, with a crew three, did vital work in outlying areas of the Western Desert, Syria and Palestine.

my going to the 'Ladies' Cabin' to report on disasters there'.

Isobel's adventure began immediately. On arrival at the docks she stood in awe of 'this huge white ship,' and 'wondered how it could possibly float. You can hardly hear any vibration from the engines,' she exclaimed. The first leg of the voyage would stop at Marseilles, Tangiers, and Gibraltar. Passengers included the terribly stiff-upper-lipped Marquis of Bute, the Duke of Westminster and pianist Harriet Cohen, who, as a result of this trip which took her to Palestine, began to support the Zionist cause for a Jewish homeland and the evacuation of Jews from Germany.

The Duke of Westminster dominated her thoughts as 'half the men on the ship have warned me to beware of his Grace,' she noted. The sea, for the most part, kept millpond-still and Isobel gushed at her first glimpse of Africa, 'The loveliest thing I've ever seen,' is how she described the sight of Tangiers' white houses and red roofs set against the blue sea and sky. In Gibraltar, the Commander invited her to see the ship enter port from the bridge, where *HMS Repulse* was preparing for a trial run before taking the King and Queen to Canada.

A stopover in Marseille left her stunned at the haphazard state of traffic. 'There are no regulations— except to give way to traffic coming from the right and two cars race for a gap and the one who loses his nerve brakes hard.'

'On the way back we saw a ship which was bombed by Franco … I must say he'd made a good job of it,' she quipped.

At that time, Marseille boasted one of the world's busiest harbours. The *SS Stratheden* sat moored near the *Viceroy of India* and *Empress of Australia*. But Isobel complained of having 'seen nothing of the fleet.' Stromboli eased her disappointment. With evident enthusiasm she described 'red hot lava running down the side into the sea and a red glow on the top [of the volcano].'

Then, back at sea and after several days of calm – pandemonium struck. 'There was an awful fuss, as bugles and sirens and rushing about. A boat drill for the crew it appears. I thought at first that Mussolini had torpedoed us!' On Sunday 18th April, the Suez Canal and Port Said homed into view, but it was a discouraging sight. 'The sea was a dirty brown colour and on the horizon was a line of buildings … no land to be seen at all.' She noted the port was a 'curious place, dirty and smelly' before boarding a train to Cairo. Isobel noted 'huge American cars going about 50 mph, donkey carts, Arabs on bicycles, cars hooting, people shouting and buses... the perfect nightmare'.

Mary and Margaret—two Naafi colleagues, who would become close friends—were on the platform and whisked Isobel off to take up residence in the *Heliopolis House Hotel*, a dilapidated building, full of army and air force officers.

A newspaper advert from 1911 for the hotel.

The hotel had opened in 1910 as one of the largest and best-equipped in the world, with over 400 bedrooms. It was built for the elite in the 'Oriental style' and boasted fine restaurants, bars, baths, and huge patio, 'whence a magnificent view of the desert is obtained.'

Its position at the height of elegance did not last long, as British and Colonial Forces used it as a billet during the *First World War*, and the ground floor was converted into a military hospital. Between the two world wars *Heliopolis House* sprang back to life as a tourist destination, but by 1939, darker times saw the return of the military, and when Isobel arrived it had become the image of fading decadence.

The Heliopolis House Hotel, used as the Naafi billet.

On that first night in the *Heliopolis* Isobel sank into a quagmire of problems as hungry mosquitoes swarmed, the heat stifled, and the constant stream of planes rising over the hotel from the nearby RAF base proved deafening. 'Well I suppose they will need all the practice they can get,' was her good-humoured response.

Nevertheless, she complained to her father that: 'It is too hot to walk anywhere—Many rumours of war these days, I just don't think about it.' Sleep-deprived and disoriented, even small incidents could cause great upset. One evening, while reading in bed, Isobel spotted an enormous cockroach running across the pillow. 'I simply leapt out of bed. Mary came running thro'. She thought somebody was murdering me.'

Delivery of the letters to her father ranged between fast to erratic, but generally, mail usually took a week to reach home.

Away from *Hell House* life was reasonably straightforward, but Isobel complained that it was impossible to get anything done between 1–4 pm, as 'all the shops were shuttered and natives lie down anywhere and sleep—I don't blame them.'

The blistering heat made work exhausting. Oppressive swarms of flies required that anything remotely comestible be covered with muslin. Even Naafi veterans complained that working in outdoor canteens under canvas in the blazing sun, was a real test for their stamina. Egypt is also plagued by a strong, dry, dust-laden wind called the *Simoom*, which, along with hot temperatures and large quantities of dust, can make life miserable.

During her first week in Egypt, Isobel organised 600 Naafi teas for a school sports day, a dance buffet for 400 attendees, and a 'picnic tea' at the Pyramids for 170 people in the middle of an afternoon, an event which clearly irked her:

> Did you ever hear of such nonsense? There wasn't an inch of shade anywhere, not even a tent and the sand was so hot that we could hardly bare to walk on it, much less sit down! I'm afraid there

would have been a strong smell of cooking flesh if anyone had attempted it.

Although the British technically led cloistered lives, they were still part of wider society, and Isobel kept a hectic social schedule, attending a seemingly endless round of cocktail parties, theatre performances, and late suppers. At the *Kursaal*, customers could wine, dine, and dance all night. The *Badia* music-hall employed a local band blaring out British tunes; as couples swayed, squeezed, leered and hugged- evenings at the *Badia* usually ended with a performer swathed in Union Jack singing *It's a long way to Tipperary*.

Another popular haunt across town, was the notoriously seedy *Kit Kat Klub* - which was always 'full of service people dancing with the ladies of the establishment.' Patrons remember the smell of incense, and dozens of cheap Persian rugs scattered on the polished floor.

Sometimes, Isobel passed quieter nights by at the river watching the sunset. It was there one evening, fresh after a fall of summer rain, that she first saw the flying boat *Caledonia* taking off for Athens and onto England, 'Alexandria to Southampton in eleven hours with mails,' she exclaimed. 'It doesn't say anything about females though! At present it takes two days and costs 40 pounds.'

The luxuriously furnished Naafi *Imperial Club* was the epicentre of military social life, with its extended library, bar, restaurant and reading room. Locally employed waiters, all wearing short starched white jackets, pressed the wine list into hundreds of hands every day. Despite being under her close scrutiny, the waiters were a constant source of exasperation for Isobel, as they displayed a 'unique talent' for breaking crockery and skiving off at any given opportunity. Some staff shrugged their shoulders when asked questions, or sipped lemonade during work time, but, between bouts of bad-tempered grousing they could be cooperative and polite.

Occasionally after work, Isobel hung around the club to watch water polo, or lounge about with a cold drink on the swimming pool terrace. In her descriptions of these leisure hours, she reveals a less than enlightened attitude toward racial matters. 'They are all as brown as niggers,' she wrote of those at the pool. 'In fact some of them are niggers as it is an international club.' Sometimes she took tea at the nearby Mena House hotel, where she avoided bathing as 'the water was simply filthy and the pool was full of fat hairy Egyptians and Jews.'

By early May, the heat was intolerable, especially at the RAF canteens in Helonan and Abbassia Garrison perched on the sandy plains outside Cairo:

> The manager here—a Maltese—has just been in to tell me that the temperature has risen to 100 F (37.7C). I believe it actually went up to 125F (51C) once. If it does that this year I shall melt. I can understand why people become so lazy abroad; you simply haven't the energy you have at home.

As summer rolled on, Isobel's letters home speculated about the possibility of war. On May 3rd, she asked her father:

> What do you think old Hitler's up to now? The general feeling here is that he has gone too far. All the Italians have been recalled from Egypt and

Greeks all to be eligible for the Egyptian army. The British fleet is in Alexandria.

A military exercise held in Cairo further stoked local anxieties, as it included a blackout, complete with gas masks and bomb effects. 'I believe that the precautions were so successful that the war was called off,' Isobel joked. The exercise was widely reported in the British press:

> A 36-hour 'state of war' for big air raid exercises, in which the British and Egyptian Armies and Air Forces are cooperating began in the Cairo area today. Troops in war equipment have taken up strategic positions in the city with fixed bayonets. Anti-aircraft guns and searchlights have been manned, and machine-guns placed on the roofs of private houses in preparation for seven air-raids by squadrons of RAF bombers. The bombers are taking off from the Western Desert, and will be attacked by British and Egyptian fighters. Tonight, a black-out to be enforced over an area of 400 square miles with 1,500,000 inhabitants. Trains and road traffic will be at a standstill. Small explosive, gas, and incendiary bombs are being detonated by police. River transport is being mobilised for a test evacuation of the population.[97]

Soon after the exercise, Isobel and Margaret accepted an

---

[97] Dundee Evening Telegraph – May 15th, 1939

invitation from Mr. and Mrs Cooper, a Naafi area manager and his wife who lived in Ismailia on the west bank of the Suez Canal.

> It is mostly French in population. Newcomers are not welcomed. The town itself is lovely. Beautiful gardens with flowering trees and beds of flowers and green grass—and when you think that the whole place is built in the desert and every blade of grass has to be watered it's quite marvellous.

As a single woman, with free bed and board, Isobel was aware of a pleasant breeziness to her everyday life. Some would even say she squandered her money away. One spending spree ended with Isobel the proud possessor of five gold teeth, at a cost of quite a few six-pence-a-week instalments. Patriotism and the persistent gossip of the danger from 'natives panicking and looting' if war broke out persisted that summer:

> Egypt is full of spies—German and Italian; a German of the species was in this hotel and only just escaped before the Police came. We do see life! Things are very unsettled here. Troops coming and going and rumours of all kinds are rife.

The occasional snippet of Naafi gossip crept into Isobel's letters. She remarked in a note written in early July, that the institute was 'hard put to find staff to cope with the conscripts' back in Britain. She also described how the problem of pilfering kept her busy: 'Just by way of variation I'm doing a commodity stock in one of the canteens. We suspect the manager of reselling our tea and sugar.'

Short deployments and vacations to neighbouring Palestine were common among Naafi staff in Egypt, but the growing menace of terrorism from Jewish extremists against the British caused Isobel to dither about plans to visit Jerusalem:

> If I get the chance of going to Palestine I'll certainly fly, as it's a wicked journey by train. No hope of that meantime, too many bombs about. I believe they have a truckload of Arabs always in front of the engine to make sure there are no bombs on the line. A cheerful thought.

In August, she interpreted a flood of Empire troops into Egypt as kindling for local squabbles. 'Looks like trouble for somebody,' she observed, after hearing that 10,000 Indian soldiers were on their way. 'If a major war does not develop there will be a small one here, between the Indians and the Egyptians! Can't see them settling down together!'[98]

The arrival of Indian troops stretched Naafi resources to the limits:

> We are not going into the desert with the troops you will be glad to hear, as there are more than enough left here to keep us busy. I have two

---

[98] On August3rd, 1939, the 11th Indian Infantry Brigade left India for Egypt as reinforcements for the British garrison. Before the end of 1939, further reinforcements had arrived in Egypt.

camps out at the Pyramids, one R.A.S.C. & the other R.H.H. with 150 Ghurkas for good measure. I'm busy on a diet sheet for the officers messing. Heaven knows what the Ghurkas eat, mostly rice I should think. Yesterday I was at the Mena Camp in the morning, right at the Pyramids but not at all romantic. We expect a further 3,000 British troops there in a week or so to be ready for an emergency.

Egypt felt mobilised even before the outbreak of war. A week prior, Isobel wrote to her father that the 'stage seems set.' Her descriptions of the tense atmosphere merit quoting at length:

Am not feeling in the least nervous for myself, daddy, being the only woman left on the staff—I just hope I shall be able to rise to the occasion and do what is required of me. At any rate I shall do my best. Probably will have to move from the hotel to barracks in the garrison. Probably my job will be to cater for the soldiers' families.

The whole thing seems too horrible to happen— but I suppose when one's time comes to die one might as well be bombed as run over in the street. Have spent one half of the morning arranging the catering and the other half cancelling the same! Nearly all the troops have gone to war stations. The garrison is empty and it feels so queer, waiting for something to happen.

Isobel decided to stay at *Hell House*, despite its location in the so-called danger zone. She assured her father, 'troops from the aerodrome could be here in five minutes if the natives riot. That is our chief danger.' Her letters from this period show her increasingly stolid response to the challenges of the place:

> We have just heard that the Mediterranean is to be closed to merchant shipping, so it looks bad. At the Naafi, there is a great fuss going on because one of the corporals has developed dysentery – everything has to be sterilised. Yesterday morning I went up to the R.A.O.C. canteen and raised hell. The place was filthy, so I stayed all morning and saw it cleaned. I'll never be afraid of cockroaches again. They simply fell off the walls and I stood on them. Later they were swept up and burnt!

Isobel closes this last letter with an interesting paragraph: 'We all think here that Adolf has got the wind up. There's no doubt about it that the Italians daren't come over here! I suppose Adolf will now proceed to save the face of Europe in his usual barefaced manner.'

When the war broke out, Isobel reacted with predictable anguish and her letters were subjected to army censors. Any information intelligence officers thought useful to the enemy was blacked out.

The upshot of this provides a slightly sketchier picture of life. Worse still, war's outbreak made up-to-date newspapers and reliable information scarce, turning Cairo became a breeding ground for gossip. 'There was a rumour last week that London had been bombed,' Isobel wrote on September 24th. She talked of borrowing a radio, which frustratingly only received 'German propaganda.'

Patchy shortwave radio made reception of the BBC difficult, with the news often impossible to decipher among the crackles and hisses. There was too a deep schism between daily life in Cairo and the exigencies of war. As Isobel observed, 'you wouldn't think that there was a war on except that the men are all in uniform, and the place is riddled with air raid shelters.'

That same week, Isobel dished out meals on a railway platform to troops passing through Cairo for the Sudan. She noted that the Naafi was, in her words, 'beginning to run short of supplies.' She was nevertheless grateful: 'I just thought the other day that I must have the only job of this kind in the world at the moment, and consider myself very lucky to have it too!'

Meanwhile, a new regulation prompted murmurs of discontent among the ranks, as cabarets, clubs and bars were deemed off-limits after 1:30AM. However, celebrations on October 19th proved an exception to this new rule as Great Britain and France won a diplomatic victory by signing a pact of mutual assistance with Turkey, allowing the Allies free access through the Dardanelles to Romania and Greece.

Wing Commander Gardiner, a close friend and part of Isobel's Cairo social circle, was at the signing ceremony. 'He brought me a brass box of the country,' she wrote on his return from Istanbul: 'He sat in my room last night and described the whole scene of the signing of the treaty. It was like something out of the Arabian Nights. I said to him, 'you've been at the making of history."

Despite the war, life plodded on. A wedding reception on November 19th aboard a *Thomas Cook* Nile steamer provided an amusing incident. During the after-party clear up, the boy responsible for washing the bar's glasses was found to have been drinking the heel taps from all the glasses. He was very drunk, and 'fell down stairs when carrying a box of china and broke the lot. He then proceeded to throw all the bits overboard, destroying the evidence. When I tackled him he said his arm was tired—doubtless from elbow bending!'

In the same letter, she added: 'We don't hear much news about the war these days. Can't understand why you are not getting my letters, unless Adolf has sunk them.' Her statement proved prophetic. By the end of 1939, peril in the Mediterranean began to impact Naafi shipments, prompting Isobel to start sourcing local foodstuffs as supplies were 'not coming through very well.'

Away from work, Isobel enjoyed golf, French lessons, and horse riding, but life at *Hell House*, however, remained trying, especially as the native servants were 'the noisiest people imaginable, even an ordinary conversation sounds like an argument.'

On 12th February, 1940, less than a year after arriving in Cairo, Isobel wrote to her father with dramatic news:

> I suppose I'd better tell you about Tony...
> He's younger than I am, to begin with, but that just can't be helped. He is also in the Naafi so we will have that interest in common. To be quite honest Daddy, he's a very average young man, with average prospects and intelligence and a large amount of understanding. I'm aware that I won't be making what is commonly thought to be a 'good match' in the material sense, but I think I am in every other way.

Meanwhile, Isobel became the proud owner of a 1934 Morris, a two-seater that boasted a new battery, new piston rings and four 'quite good' tyres. But: 'The brakes will have to be seen to, there is no hood, no horn and I think it's been on fire once.' She conceded that the car would suffice 'for running in and out of Cairo and round the camps.'

Friday, May 10th, 1940 was one of the most dramatic days in British history. Winston Churchill's ascension to PM had the government in disarray. On the continent, Germany ended the *Phoney War* by invading the Low Countries. Mixing serious political observation with dry humour, Isobel wrote of the news:

> We are all frightfully interested in the new war cabinet. Poor old Neville[99]—I'm rather sorry for him, but he wasn't the man for the job. What do you think of Winston? It's just unfortunate that we didn't have him years ago. After all he has been telling us for years to prepare and now he gets the baby to hold.

Tony and Isobel married in Cairo on August 23rd 1940. Their happy new life was interrupted soon after when Tony was sent to Palestine, stoically, she called this pause in their relationship, 'the fortune or misfortune of war.' With Tony away, Isobel and Mary decided to work longer hours, given that theirs was a reserved occupation which prevented them from joining the ARP:

> The most useful thing is to tuck into our own job. I can't help thinking that we have all become too pleasure loving and even now we don't realise that it's going to take everything we've got to win this war—win we shall, but it will be a bitter struggle.

When Tony returned in the middle of 1941, the country

---

[99] Neville Chamberlain

was a hive of military activity with Naafi nearly bursting under the strain. Isobel wrote on October 1st that, 'we don't see much of our home these days as we are usually out catering 5 nights a week.' With so much troop movement, news from around the region poured in:

> Ben White, a friend of ours also in Naafi, has just come back from Tobruk. He's been there for a year and so it was time he was relieved. He spends his time having baths to make up for the ones he has missed! He keeps us amused with tales of his doings in the besieged garrison! War caused acute shipping shortages.

The menace of German U-boats meant that imports of essential goods into Egypt began to slow. Local produce helped to fill shortages, however:

> We are very lucky here, tho' things are expensive we don't go short – except for potatoes, which are now more precious than gold! Everything very expensive here and getting daily more so, but still we are lucky. We have two meatless days a week now, but the vegetables are good and cheap so we don't suffer. Macaroni is my great standby. I'm qualifying for the army of occupation in Italy!

There were even the occasional treats, such strawberries from the Sudan and locally produced marmalade. In January of 1942, the Naafi chairman arrived in Cairo to inspect operations, when he suggested more restaurant superintendents were required – his comment annoyed Isobel, who brushed it off as a 'most unsatisfactory arrangement.'

Mary and I don't like the idea at all. Being the only two English women on the staff we have a very good time, thoroughly spoilt! But I can't see any of the local ladies working like we do. However we'll see what happens.

That summer saw Isobel and Mary briefly transferred to Jerusalem. The two set off at the crack of dawn on a blistering June morning, 'all stocked up with iron rations in case we have to spend a night in the desert.' But the trip was short and it wasn't long before Isobel was back in Egypt organising a cocktail party for ENSA boss Basil Dean, who was entertaining the press. 'Tonight we are going to a show in which Josephine Baker figures,' she wrote. 'I wonder if she'll be allowed to do her usual act!'[100]

Middle East operations resumed a semblance of normality when Germany was neutralized in late 1943 and supplies of food and fuel began to arrive as the Royal Navy regained dominance of the Mediterranean.

The closing months of the war brought together staffers for reunions in Cairo.

Many returned with extraordinary stories. One Naafi driver told an incredible tale of being cut off during the retreat to Alamein. He struck out into the desert and drove for 36 hours, completely lost. The driver kept going until, eventually, to his great surprise, he found himself in

---

[100] Josephine Baker was an entertainer and during her early career she was renowned as a dancer, and was among the most celebrated performers to headline the revues of the Folies Bergère in Paris.

sight of the Pyramids. Another driver fell into German hands and was questioned by an intelligence officer. He posed as a Red Cross man and claimed he didn't know how to drive. A few hours later he escaped with his canteen and a week's supply of petrol pilfered from enemy dump.

Isobel and Tony's Egyptian adventure came to an end along with 1943. They were given a permanent posting to Palestine, where her duties shifted from catering to welfare, looking after the civilian waitresses, chambermaids, and cooks.

This job meant frequent travel to Haifa, although Isobel claimed to 'enjoy the jaunts and seeing a bit of the country.' She also hoped to see Cyprus, which fell within her district, 'but not in the winter thank you!' She complained that conditions in Palestine were 'much more wartime' than in Egypt and that 'the cost of living is appalling.' She reckoned that 'housekeeping is going to be a nightmare—but it is worth it for the sake of the climate.'

The birth of her first child in 1944 saw Isobel sign-off work. She described the baby, christened Dick, as a 'sturdy little trout' who was 'going to be a strapping lad.' There were some issues with procurement: 'Can't get a pram—so am fixing him up with an orange box, padded inside with a sheepskin cover for the winter so he ought to be as snug as a bug!'

With Isobel at home, Tony became the sole breadwinner, but making ends meet became a struggle and domestic life could be testing.

> Tony's clerk in the office decamped with the petty cash, the small amount of 200 pounds, and two days ago when some workmen were blasting the

rock in our back garden to make a cess pit, a stone fell on a woman's head and killed her. I may add that the nursery window overlooks this and is just 50 yards away—so now I keep the shutters closed.

I am still considering going back to the office as the cost of living is appalling and though we live very simply, it is difficult to make both ends meet. If I could find a good girl for Dick I wouldn't hesitate.

Isobel eventually returned to work, life in Palestine, though, was becoming 'a bit tricky' as the relative wartime calm came to an end. The publication of a *White Paper* in 1939 had ratcheted up anti-British sentiment. The document outlined new government policies restricting Jewish immigration and a ten-year plan for an independent, Arab-majority Palestine. The fight against Nazi Germany had calmed the volatile atmosphere in Palestine between 1940 and 1944, but once Germany was defeated, old tensions returned. An increase in terrorist assassinations, abductions, and bombings (both Jewish and Arab) curtailed careers and endangered thousands of British lives, including those of Isobel and Tony:

We have just moved again as you will see from the new address. It was all done in a great hurry and we are hardly settled in the new house. We now live in a camp called Sarafand, down on the plain. It is very hot and sticky and we miss the cool nights in Jerusalem. Tony has been very busy as Air Vice Marshall Brooke-Popham has been round inspecting canteens. He got a few rockets from the troops about Singapore I'm afraid! However he was satisfied with what he saw apparently.

By June 1946, Isobel, Tony, and Dick were ready to return to the United Kingdom. The family packed up and left on the Matuka – New Zealand line. Her final letter from Palestine informed her father that the journey was meant to take:

> 10 – 11 days and so far we don't know where we dock. You might find it Lloyds shipping lists in the Herald but we'll send you a cable as soon as we know. We ought to be home in two weeks. After all this time I can hardly believe it.

As it happened, Isobel, Tony and Dick were sailing out of a storm, as the situation in Palestine rapidly deteriorated.

CHAPTER 15
PALESTINE

WHEN ships transporting British POWs from Singapore and Malaya home arrived at Suez, their first stop on the 12,000-mile journey to freedom, they found Naafi awaiting with a 400-yard-long free buffet, decorated like a carnival.

For troops ending their tour in Egypt, their limbo-period was eased at the new Naafi 'Palm Beach' holiday camp at Sidi Bishr, dubbed by visitors 'Egypt's Miami Beach.' The 10,000 service men and women that checked-in could only be thankful that they were heading home, as the situation in neighbouring Palestine was becoming untenable, with increasing terrorism amid the slow ebb of British regional control.

On July 22nd, 1946, a bomb planted by the Jewish *Irgun* organisation exploded at the *King David Hotel*, the British civil and military headquarters in Jerusalem.

It was one of history's most brutal acts of political violence. The five-storey building collapsed like a pack of cards with 200 British, Arabs, and Jews inside. Terrorists dressed as Palestinian Arabs had hidden explosives in milk churns and secreted them to the hotel basement.

By this time, the formidable figure of Colonel Harvey Swithenbank - a well-connected and respected member of the organisation had been appointed the region's Naafi commander.

His wife Anne was employed as a secretary with the British government in Jerusalem, eventually holding the dubious distinction of being the last British civilian woman to leave Palestine.

Swithenbank received his baptism of fire that day at the *King David Hotel.* As smoke and fire billowed from the ruins, Swithenbank—one of the first men on the scene—frantically dug barehanded through the rubble for survivors.

Sir John Shaw, chief secretary of the Palestine Government, who himself narrowly escaped death, expressed his grief in a broadcast message:

> The majority of the dead and wounded were my own staff, many of whom I have known personally for eleven years. Their only crime was their devoted, unselfish, and impartial service to Palestine and its peoples. For this, they have been rewarded by cold-blooded mass murder.

The attack killed 91 people. The depleted secretariat moved to an improvised office in a *YMCA* building opposite the ruined hotel.

The event marked the end of the pleasant, cosmopolitan existence enjoyed by the tripartite community of Jerusalem. Naafi, as a central component of the military occupation, became a target and suffered many attacks.

A newspaper correspondent noted: 'Now its life is tuned to a painful pitch of nervousness. The people are jumpy and quick-tempered. The sound of a lorry back-firing makes hearts skip a beat…'

One month after the King David bombing, a similar explosion destroyed the booking hall and Naafi premises at Haifa railway station.

The *King David Hotel* in Jerusalem after the blast. (Authors private collection).

Two separate ambushes the following week seriously wounded a Quartermaster Sergeant of the *Sixth Airborne Division* and a Naafi girl. Soon after, a landmine destroyed a Naafi truck at a level crossing near the town of Hadera, luckily the driver escaped with minor injuries.

Naafi at Gaza 1945 (Authors private collection)

The evacuation from Palestine began in February 1947, as nearly 2,000 British women, children, and non-essential men departed Jerusalem, Haifa, Tel-Aviv, and Jaffa. All civilian Naafi employees were ordered to live in barracks. Tensions grew further when an explosion at the *Goldsmith Officers' Club* in Jerusalem killed nine Naafi workers, two British officers, one British soldier, and a police officer. Harvey Swithenbank narrowly escaped that atrocity, having left the club just hours before.

In the early part of 1947, Naafi kept about 300 British women in Palestine, working in Hadera, Tel Levinsky, Gaza, Akia, Isdud and Khassa, as well as in Jerusalem and Sarafand.

But the appalling security situation required this number be reduced, with most leaving by summer. The twelve who remained were evacuated by air to Egypt the following year. Swithenbank said:

The ATS/EFI girls have been absolutely magnificent ever since the troubles began. I cannot really say enough for their unfailing loyalty and excellent behaviour all through. We'd have been quite lost without their help—not only in offices but in clubs and canteens. None of them ever asked for a posting, despite the life behind the wire, and I never once heard them complain. I should like to thank the girls, one and all, for their really grand example.

This end spelled victory for the terrorists and Britain relinquished Palestine to the United Nations in 1947. Stanley Baker, the Manager of the Naafi Overseas Canteen Service, paid a final visit to Palestine at the beginning of 1948. His notes, titled 'last look round before the bloodbath' make grim-reading.

As I write, the curtain rises on the last tragic act in the Palestine drama. Even before these words are read, that unhappy land may be aflame with the blazing hatreds of Arabs and Jews, no longer held in check by British control. In January this year, I made what will probably be my final duty tour of Palestine. I brought back a confused picture of a country falling to pieces day by day; a land of growing lawlessness, of mounting hatreds, of Arabs and Jews, becoming ever more audacious, ever more ruthless, and with a steady breakdown of communications, transport, industry and all the ordinary amenities of life.[101]

---

[101] Naafi News, Summer, 1948.

Unrest had taken the lives of 140 British soldiers and police officers, along with dozens of civilian bystanders.

Naafi's 27-year association with Palestine ended on June 30th, 1948, without ceremony, when the last EFI officer, Captain George Taylor, left by sea from Haifa.

CHAPTER 16
RETURN TO GERMANY

REBUILDING Britain after the devastation of *World War Two* would be nothing short of a miracle. The piled-up remains of destroyed houses, factories, shops, and churches lead to one of the biggest reconstruction efforts the world had known, after the seemingly endless barrage of destruction inflicted on London, Birmingham, Portsmouth, Plymouth, Coventry and Hull.

The future belonged to the prefab, according to the Housing Minister, as he praised new prefabricated emergency housing, which was made in sections so small that they could be dropped off on the back of a lorry.

Victory had left Britain insolvent for the first time in its history, costing the nation a quarter of its wealth. Never before had so much been lost and in addition to the repair of damaged infrastructure, the new Labour government, headed by Clement Atlee, faced the prospect of demobilising nine million men and the reinvigoration industry and business. Lord Keynes, the government financial advisor, called it a 'financial Dunkirk'.

For Naafi, the changes were immediate, as at once many garrisons and RAF stations suddenly were left deserted. The day after the war ended, the first Naafi branches shut their doors at Scapa Flow and across east Scotland, but given the parlous state of the economy, it is remarkable that 120,000 people were still on the payroll during the summer of 1945. Vast quantities of surplus Naafi furniture was sold-off to over 5,000 catering houses in Bridlington, Cleethorpes, Blackpool, Fleetwood,

Morecombe and Skegness. Other items went to *Berwick Holiday Camp*, which was converted from RAF quarters into a modern tourist centre within in a month of VE Day.

Chairman Lancelot Royle gave a brief comment about the prospects for the Naafi in peacetime:

> The future? That depends on the post-war size of our forces—a Cabinet matter. In the next few years, there will reduction to about one-third Naafi's present size. Much more of the food purchases will branded goods from British manufacturers. But we shall need the best brains of our staff to help us the coming years of adjustment.[102]

Gradually, Naafi transferred some canteens and clubs— mostly in northwest Europe—from military to civilian operations. In July, 36 Naafi girls arrived by air in Oslo to serve troops there, whilst more staff arrived in Vienna, which was considered an increasingly important posting.

It was there that nine-million cigarettes, thousands of cases of whisky, brandy, gin and tons of chocolate were destroyed in a Naafi depot fire in late 1945- but, thanks to Captain William Swan, the 29-year-old area chief, troops did not go short of their luxuries for more than 48 hours as while the fire was still in progress, Swan arranged for complete replenishment of the destroyed stocks to be sent from Klagenfurt, whilst his assistant Sergt. Clifford Grice organised the local firefighting squads, and managed to save a large quantity of stock.

Back in Britain, surplus stocks continued being disposed

---

[102] The Herald, January 2nd, 1946

of via sales to government departments, retailers, hospitals, restaurants, and councils. For Rhoda Woodward, the closure of the Naafi where she had spent the war was an unforgettable moment.

> At last, it all ended. We all gathered on the airfield, Officers, Airmen and W.A.A.F.'s for an open-air service, and as the camps closed, we all went back to a very much changed 'Civvie Street'. Things would never be quite the same again.

As clubs in France, Holland, Italy and Belgium wound down, posts in the Far East, including at Singapore and Hong Kong, saw influx. Egypt once again became the hub of British military activity, overseeing naval and air commands across the Middle East and Mediterranean.

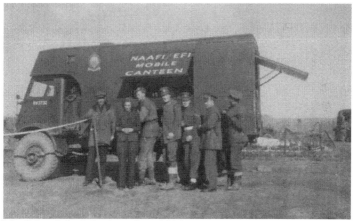

Naafi break in Salonica, circa 1946

Meanwhile, new 'luxury' Naafi clubs had begun to

spring up across Britain in the latter years of the war, providing well-stocked libraries, quiet reading and writing-rooms, as well as taverns, games-rooms, cafeterias, baths, religious services, debates and lectures.

The first two new clubs were showcased in Manchester and Southampton, with others in Nottingham, Darlington, Aberdeen, Doncaster, Plymouth, Lincoln, Carlisle, Chester, and Sleaford opening soon after.

The average club could accommodate up to 1,000 people and service uniform was the only passport needed to get in. However, the new clubs also attracted stunningly sharp comment from some servicemen, including Pte J. Page, who observed:

> Many of us feel that these clubs—five years late, are only springing into being because of the question which arose the national papers a year or so ago as to what happens to the profits—and not because of any real desire on the part of Naafi to minister to the Forces' comfort.[103]

> These places are certainly super, as far as fittings and furnishings go...but and this is important, the same attitude of the men prevails as in the ordinary Naafi's—the take it or leave it attitude.

---

[103] Pte J. Page, letter to the *Lincolnshire Echo*, June 28th, 1945. Naafi Chief Press and Public Relations Officer Claude F Luke responded: "In common fairness, it should be stated that in the early years of the war Naafi was more than fully engaged in meeting its primary commitment— that of providing canteens on all naval, military and air stations at home and overseas."

For all its comfort; I, and many others would rather go to the little *YMCA* next door to the Lincoln Naafi and will always go—for there the leader is interested in us human beings and individuals, also his very charming voluntary lady.

***

The War ended with a slew of high-profile departures from the ranks of ENSA. Even though its leader Basil Dean was often described as one or British theatre's greatest champions, his war-time creation faced a barrage of criticism concerning accounting irregularities, dubious contracts, lewd comics, poor performances and exorbitant expense claims.

The vice-president, Sir Herbert Dunnico, described working with Dean as being like 'an absolute dictatorship' whilst accusing him of wasting public funds. The accusation left staff reeling and lead to Dean's personal private secretary resigning in sympathy with Sir Herbert saying: 'Nothing would give me greater pleasure than to resume my work for the troops in a new regime.' Dean seemed perplexed by the accusations of waste, and insisted that Naafi and Treasury watchdogs were at Drury Lane the whole time and 'not a single item escapes their scrutiny.'

Then, senior official Archie de Bear resigned, telling the media 'Drury Lane must liberated'. Matters worsened when Colonel Eric Dunstan, another a high ranking ENSA figure, also threw in the towel, saying he could not agree with the way Dean ran the organisation: 'there were serious differences of opinion, and I found the situation growing intolerable.' Although there were calls for an inquiry into the reasons for the criticisms and complaints of the working of ENSA, Herbert Morrison, the then President of the Council, refused to take action.

In a letter to his son Martin toward the end of the war, Dean appeared bitter – and suggested that his recompense from ENSA was minimal- especially as he had given up the whole of his time to organising national service entertainments.

> Dear Martin,
>
> I enclose a cheque for your birthday: not a large one, but the best I can do. Contrary to the belief of some people, this job that I am doing for the war, huge though it is, leaves me just a little poorer each month. [104]

It was a sad ending for an organisation that gave a roll call of stars their first showbiz break. Max Bygraves, Tommy Cooper, Charlie Drake, Dick Emery, Tony Hancock, Peter Sellers, Eric Sykes, Terry-Thomas and Norman Wisdom all started out on a garrison theatre stages.

Joan Laurie, then a 16- year-old soubrette, said working with ENSA was one of the most unusual experiences of her life.

> In the factories, we would do a show in the canteen at lunchtime and another at midnight. In-between it could be a hospital ward and a searchlight site. The smallest audience we ever played to was on a lighthouse on the northeast coast. Our pianist played the accordion while we

---

[104] Letter from Basil Dean to his son Martin, undated, presumably written in late 1944 (Authors private collection.)

performed on the interior steps to just two the lighthouse keeper and his daughter.[105]

75, SOUTH LODGE,
CIRCUS ROAD,
S? JOHN'S WOOD, N.W.8.

PRIMROSE 0901.

Dear Martin,

I enclose a cheque for your birthday: not a large one but the best I can do. Contrary to the belief of some people this job that I am doing for the war, huge though it is, leaves me just a little bit poorer each month . . . . . . I shall be very happy to see you whenever you get leave, or when I happen to be ...... The above telephone no. will find

In a letter to his son Martin toward the end of the war, Dean appeared bitter. (Authors private collection).

---

[105] The Stage – 9th November, 1995

The final act was left to comedian Tommy Trinder - a standard bearer for the organisation - who changed his catchphrase in August 1946, just for once, saying: 'You unlucky people!' to an audience somewhere in Burma, then the curtain rang down forever. One of the artists in that last performance later said:

> Whatever they might say about Basil Dean, ENSA looked after the song-and-dance people-very well. The pay was very good and I was even able to save money because meals and accommodation were free. Mind you, it was terribly hard work. Dancing is the last thing you wanted to do on an open-air stage in the airless oven heat surrounded by flies.[106]

With ENSA gone, the Forces were largely obliged to fall back on their own resources, with movies playing an increasing part in such entertainment. The 'RAF Cinema Corporation' became the relevant body on the air side; whilst from the War Office, the *Army Kinematograph Corporation* was born. For troops abroad, the *Forces Broadcasting Service* also began transmitting their own radio programmes, whilst also relaying the BBC. Another exciting scheme began after experiments with feather-weight discs and lightweight recording equipment. News agencies reported:

> The service will work like this: recording machines with trained operators will be available near to the forward areas as possible, and also in

---

[106] The Stage, August 31st, 1989.

the large Naafi clubs in Rome, Naples, Algiers, Cairo, and Alexandria; others will tour the main Service hospitals. Any British Serviceman or woman will be able to go to a special room in Naafi club and record a message home.

If present plans mature, thousands of British homes will be thrilled to hear the actual voices of their men and women-folk serving overseas, brought to them on miniature discs which can be played on any gramophone radiogram.

Once preparations were completed, Naafi inaugurated the *Voices of the Forces* scheme in Italy and North Africa and 10,000 messages were sent every week. The small brown discs were then the lightest gramophone records in the world—with their covering envelope; they weighed less than half-an-ounce and measured just five inches in diameter.

***

In Europe, Germany became Naafi's new priority. After the surrender of the *Third Reich,* the country was split into four occupation sectors and Berlin into four zones. The USA, USSR, United Kingdom and France held supreme authority, whilst the Commanders-in–Chiefs of the occupying powers wielded almost absolute power across the land.

On arrival in Hamburg, the new occupiers attempted to feed a population delirious with hunger, while also battling a plague of rats infesting bombed-out ruins. Allied raids had levelled seventy-seven percent of the metropolis and in the midst of this devastation, airborne Naafi surveyors descended on the city to find suitable locations for new establishments.

Meanwhile, the British Military Government, along with the Control Commission, embarked on the wholesale requisitioning of any usable buildings.[107]

The Naafi earmarked the plush harbour-side *Atlantic Hotel* for its Officers Club, whilst the famous *Laeiszhalle* concert hall—once Hamburg's cultural centre—was taken over by the *British Forces Service*. Arthur Askey and Vera Lynn records echoed where great composers such as Richard Strauss and Igor Stravinsky once played.

Local Germans, barred from the promenade at *New Jungfernstieg*, stood aghast as British soldiers nailed a 'Piccadilly Circus' sign to a building on the *Grosser Allee* - one of Hamburg's oldest commercial streets.

The Atlantic Hotel, Hamburg (photo: Nathan Morley)

---

[107] Thirteen engineers and architects sent from London supervised the work of local engineers.

After endless searching, the Naafi managed to secure the use of an immense blackened shell on *Dammtorstrasse* for their prized project. In a previous life, it had been the largest cinema in Europe. This nine-storey 'Ufa-Palast' building was the venue of choice for Nazi propaganda films, having hosted Leni Riefenstahl's 'Olympia' in 1938 and the premiere of the anti-Semitic hate film *Jud Suss* in 1940. Though left semi-derelict by an air raid, renovations offered British soldiers 'every conceivable facility' including a pub, shop, restaurant, social club and dance hall. Without regard to German sensibilities, Naafi added their pennyworth to the humiliation of the locals; by naming their new establishment the *Victory Club*.

Naafi managed to secure the use of an immense blackened shell on Dammtorstrasse for the *Victory Club*. The building is still there today. (Photo: Nathan Morley).

'The bar there was packed every night with tables weighed down by foaming glasses,' recalled 20-year-old

RAF equipment assistant Maurice Rattigan. Like most other new recruits, he arrived on boats crammed with fully-kitted soldiers, hurled and rocked by gale force winds in the North Sea.

The small fleet - shuttling between Harwich and the Hook of Holland - was dirty and uncomfortable.

Toilets backed-up as sea-sick soldiers queued to vomit, leaving an unimaginable stench. 'I had grown up in the slums,' actor Michael Caine once remarked of his own troopship experience, 'but I had never heard of a ship that had a slum area.' The *Naval Canteen Service* sold luxuries during the transports, but with most potential customers violently seasick, business proved slow.

An equally grim scene welcomed troops after disembarkation. New arrivals fanned out on trains across a devastated landscape. Their camps dotted a ruined north-west Germany.

For those posted to Hamburg, booze-fuelled evenings in the *Victory Club* provided a temporary respite from the harshness. Packed with troops from across Britain and the Empire, there was a constant struggle to resolve the dialectical conflicts, whilst drinking beer and making merry. "I visited Hamburg several times on duty," said Private Bill Cheall, serving with the Green Howard's. 'The destruction was unbelievable… Hamburg alone paid the penalty for the suffering of Coventry. It had been avenged.'

Life under occupation was a constant struggle. Everything required a permit—from crossing bridges to entering certain sections of the city, at every turn locals were rebuffed with signs declaring: 'Out of Bounds for German Civilians,' or 'For British Forces Only.' Maurice Rattigan recalled, 'Every commodity was in short supply, especially food, coffee, chocolate, and cigarettes. We couldn't help [the Germans] with food, but we could certainly sell them chocolate and cigarettes.'

For Joan King, then in her early 20s, her posting to the Naafi *Victory Club* in 1946 proved unforgettable and required near-constant vigilance as 'everything that moved got nicked.'

'Don't forget [the Germans] were starving; they weren't pinching really, they were kind of getting food,' she said, adding that some staff were sympathetic to their plight. However, thefts became so chronic, that in 1947, fifty-two members of Hamburg's biggest gang of thieves were arrested for targeting Naafi stores.

Newspapers reported a highly organised gang of 'businessmen and discharged prisoners of war,' specialised in raiding Naafi storage depots. It is reckoned that post-war black marketeers cost taxpayers £20million flogging stolen Naafi stock to Germans. Renowned journalist Ferdinand Tuohy described the Black Market as a 'menace to world society,' and during an investigation into the phenomenon, was offered a whole pig for a used tire in Denmark and butter at the rate of 1lb for twenty cigarettes.

In Germany, he 'could have got a share in a farmyard for a suit of English tweeds.' And, whilst acknowledging the gravity of the black market in Berlin, he played down the role of Allied soldiers in it.

> One aspect, however, does require to be seen in a more just focus, and that is the role played by the armies of occupation, principally the Americans and British, because they get issued with the most negotiable or 'floggable' items such as cigarettes, chocolate, canned food and other PX and Naafi commodities. While it is quite true that nearly all

ranks have aggravated the ill, and those half-hearted attempts to hinder their feeding the black market have failed, what the troops flog is a small affair when taken beside activities in the European black market as a whole.

In the first months of occupation, the Naafi toiled to keep a steady supply of cigarettes and beer flowing.

Just as they had after the *First World War*, breweries were opened locally, which supplemented the truckloads of bottled beer arriving weekly to water clubs, canteens and shops which had sprung up in Bielefeld, Brunswick, Celle, Dortmund, Düsseldorf, Gutersloh, Hanover, Herford, Krefeld, Munster, Osnabruck, Hameln, Luneburg and Oldenburg. In Rattenkrug, the 14th century *Hamelin Inn*, reputed to have been connected with the legend of the Pied Piper, was taken over as a Naafi club for warrant officers and sergeants, and new mobile vans were used as travelling shops for outlying detachments.

For some troops, the only solace from the daily drudgery came during evenings at the clubs. Sameness dominated their days. Fraternizing with Germans was strictly forbidden, however, some could not resist the temptations of a country teeming with pretty frauleins and young war widows. A fraternisation decree issued by Bernard Montgomery - who was by then the Commander of British Forces in Germany - was plastered on every Naafi and barrack notice board:

> In streets, houses, cafes, cinemas etc, you must keep clear of Germans, man, woman, and child unless you meet them in the course of your duty...In short, you must not fraternise with Germans at all.

Just prior to the occupation, an extraordinary document titled: *Instructions for British Servicemen in Germany* was distributed to educate soldiers on a range of topics. It advised:

> Wherever you are stationed in Germany you will find at first that there is practically nothing to buy. Food, clothing and tobacco will be severely rationed, there will be no little things you can send home as gifts, the shops will be empty. Your needs will be looked after by Army, Navy and RAF issue and Naafi stores. The only thing you can buy from the Germans will be a glass of beer or wine.

> Entertainment will be provided for you by ENSA in your own camp or barracks and most German places of entertainment will be out of bounds.

> The Germans are not good at controlling their feelings. They have a streak of hysteria. You will find that Germans may often fly into a passion if some little thing goes wrong. Don't be too ready to listen to stories told by attractive women. They may be acting under orders.

Rumours of discreet 'rendezvous' between soldiers and German women proved so horrifying for one priest in Newcastle, that he lamented to his local paper: 'Is it not with a sense of sheer amazement and a deep shame that we read and hear of the desire of some of our serving lads in the Forces to fraternise with the people of Nazi Germany?'

The Reverend Ernest Mitchell added that many 'thousands of mothers and fathers in this country are similarly perplexed.'

When twenty-eight Naafi girls arrived in Hamburg that summer, they immediately became the 'world's most sought-after women.' The *Liverpool Evening Express* described troops, denied feminine company under the non-fraternisation order, giving the new girls a tremendous welcome.

The demand for Naafi girls for parties, walks, and dances was so high, that a system was introduced whereby each girl had to be signed for before a soldier took her out.

Meanwhile, 250 kilometres south-east of Hamburg, British, French and American forces were setting up their own occupation zones in Berlin. When the Western Allies moved into Berlin in June 1945 to replace Soviet troops in western sectors, the mighty 7th Armoured Division took the central role in the British occupation. They were joined by the American 2nd Armoured division and the First French Army.

Persuading the Soviet Union to provide transit routes for Western Forces proved tough, but eventually, three routes were agreed.

Western Allies considered unrestricted access to Berlin a natural right of occupation, the Russians however, exploited Berlin's isolated position in the middle of their occupation zone to circumscribe this right.

Finally, British Forces established the Brooke, Haig, Montgomery, Alexander, Wavell, and Smuts barracks, along with Gatow airfield on the western edge of the city in Spandau.

Amerika Haus / Summit House today. (Photo: Nathan Morley)

The Naafi *Works and Buildings Branch* wasted no time in converting the former *Amerika Haus* on the corner of *Adolf Hitler-Platz* into a club 'worthy of the British troops in Berlin, upon whom rest the eyes of American, French, Russians, and other Allied powers stationed in the Metropolis. The Naafi Club's red neon sign beaconed all within twenty miles every night.'

Naafi Public Relations sent out a note to journalists, describing the exciting scene:

> From its many windows one overlooks ruined Berlin down the famous two-mile Kaiserdamm, originally built for the parade of Nazi armies and over to the blitzed Olympic Stadium towards the autobahn leading away to Brunswick, Hanover, and the west.

Accounts hail the resourceful Naafi construction team, as the *Amerika Haus* had been severely damaged in a 1943 bombing raid and needed a total renovation.

Completely lacking new construction materials, Naafi launched a huge scavenging operation among the ruins. Builders took marble slabs from Herman Goring's Air Ministry, Hitler's Chancellery and Ribbentrop's private residence. The Naafi Club's front door came from the Gestapo Headquarters. Engineers liberated kitchen, water, and heating equipment from German Officers' Messes. Ornate marble, imported by the Nazis from Italy, decorated the club's main entrance.

The Naafi was predictably proud of their achievement. A press release noted that 'insulating slabs for the refrigerating rooms came from the Oranienburg concentration camp near Berlin (Sachsenhausen), where Nazis carried out temperature experiments on human beings and war materials.'

The Club's lower floors housed a 750 seat theatre decked out with equipment and wooden stage taken from the *Kroll Opera House*—the very same platform from which Hitler had declared war on the United States in 1941.

In total, 600 workers toiled on the project. When completed, the club boasted 27 bathrooms, massage and 'sunray' rooms, a lounge, shops, two phone boxes (for UK and Northern Ireland service), a beer tavern, a concert hall, an exhibition hall, a restaurant, a cafe, a ladies lounge, reading and writing rooms, a library, games rooms and a roof terrace.

Royal Air Force Marshall and Commander in Chief of the British Forces of Occupation, Sir Sholto Douglas, cut the ribbon on Thursday, August 1st, 1946 with a party that recalled pre-war days.

Famous conductor Geraldo and his band played alongside impressionist Mandie Edwards and ventriloquist Peter Brough (of *Educating Archie* fame) who also flew in from London. Troops delighted in their new club on that opening night. Proceedings, however, came to a sudden and anti-climactic end when the bar shut at 10.30pm. Kicking-out time, even for occupying British forces, was strictly enforced.

Not all was parties, though. Eileen Taylor felt doubt over her new job as a Naafi girl within 15 minutes of her arrival in Berlin. 'The children had swollen stomachs...the Germans...picked up cigarette ends dropped by our soldiers...Every morning you saw women picking through the dustbins for our leftovers,' she remembered. Taylor was billeted in a small flat which had been used by the Gestapo, which still had spy holes in the doors.

Occasionally, she worked at a shop on the outskirts of Berlin, in Grunewald, where the only saleable stock was Wellington boots and liberty bodices. 'There were no display stands ... so we used gin bottles.'

Taylor also worked at other canteens in the city, including one on the famed *Kurfurstendamm* at the old *Kabaret der Komiker* – this was renamed the 'Winston Club' and its opening by Churchill himself in 1945 was witnessed by a reporter from *The People* newspaper:

> The Premier, who was in radiant form, had a great welcome from troops when he went to the Kurfurstendamm, Berlin's Piccadilly, to open the Naafi centre which has been named after him. When Churchill entered the club, with Field-Marshals Montgomery and Alexander and his daughter Mary, the troops opened up with "For

he's a jolly good fellow," and gave him three great cheers. When Churchill left the Naafi Club, a crowd of people broke through the military cordon, smiling, clapping and shouting 'Hurrah for Churchill.' The Premier, looking a bit flustered, gave the V-sign. It happened in Berlin today, and the crowd were Germans.[108]

The old *Kabaret der Komiker* – this was named the 'Winston Club'. Today it is a gym and a Turkish restaurant. (Photo: Nathan Morley).

Thirty-five miles south-west of Berlin at the UFA film studios in Potsdam, a central supply depot was set-up in the building where Marlene Dietrich had filmed *The Blue Angel* fifteen years earlier.

Naafi transformed the studio commissary into *The*

---

[108] The People, July 22nd, 1945

Elstree Arms canteen – referencing the famous British film studios.

Naafi set up the *Elstree Arms* in the UFA film studio in Babelsberg, near Potsdam. The building survives, as seen above in 2018. (Photo: Nathan Morley).

Nearby, nestled deep in lush green woodland, three lakeside cafes served coffee and cakes. Inspired by infamous booze-fuelled parties held for demobbed troops, one of the cafes came to be called the *Café De Mob*, whilst another provided a full range of water-sports, fishing gear and even trips on a Naafi pleasure steamer, as the *Daily Mirror* reported on 25th July 1945:

> Naafi is running a showboat for British troops in Berlin; she will take 350 soldiers on her first cruise on Havel See, one of Berlin's great lakes today. Beer, tea and cakes will be served by German

waitresses, destined later to wear 'navy' uniform with bell-bottomed trousers and sailor caps bearing the Naafi badge. The pleasure steamer, to be named *Pettit's Packet* after Major Pettit, commanding Naafi in Berlin, will be christened by Junior Commander Mary Churchill. Then, ENSA will give a performance of 'Blitz and Pieces' under the spacious covered passenger deck.

***

This period flags up another interesting tale, found in a vast collection of formerly top-secret files held at the *National Archives* in London.

It concerns twenty-eight-year-old Naafi canteen worker Sergeant Arthur Chapple, who British military police described as having a 'Yorkshire accent and a cringing and servile manner.' MPs launched a citywide hunt across Berlin for him in the summer of 1945.

It transpired that at the outbreak of the war, Chapple had joined the first Naafi troops in France, but was picked up by the Germans in Doullens and sent to a POW camp in Germany.

He became instantly unpopular, gaining a reputation as a habitual moaner. To make matters worse, he spoke fluent German and was often seen nattering with the camp guards, an avocation that did not raise his status among the other inmates.

The biggest deprivation for prisoners was having no news from the outside world, so when an illegal radio used by British POWs was discovered at the camp, rumours circulated that Chapple had tipped off the Germans. Shunned and persecuted, any loyalty Chapple may have had for Britain evaporated. He bitterly resented his treatment and threw his lot in with the Nazis, offering his services as a writer for a German magazine 'The Camp.' He had, according to his interrogation reports, spent sometime working as a correspondent for a newspaper in Leeds during the 30s, probably the *Wakefield Times*.

Arthur Chapple's Prisoner of War card

After fleeing to the enemy side, he was coaxed behind the microphone and instructed to read and write radio scripts aimed at demoralizing the British public.

He helped produce a constant diet of propaganda in the German state-controlled *Radio National*. At one point, he even lived in the same building as William Joyce, also known as *Lord Haw Haw*, the star turn of the Nazi propaganda machinery. Chapple later joined the *British Free Corps*- a Nazi organization designed for action against the Russian partisans operating behind German lines.

His collaboration gave him the freedom to roam Berlin at will, draw a salary of 400 DM per month and enjoy a reasonably busy and unhindered social life.

Yet, unlike *Haw Haw*, Chappel never threatened his listeners with bombings or taunted them about their wives' straying. His on-air character was a malcontent northerner giving talks from a 'working man's point of view.'

Joyce wrote many of his scripts, and Chapple hammed up his thick Yorkshire accent, ending up sounding like a dead ringer for Compo from the sitcom *Last of the Summer Wine*. Still, his tone was friendly, almost conversational, albeit sinister in what it conveyed. 'Can anybody be fooled by t'Jewish—Plutocratic agitating lies?' he asked in a 1943 broadcast, monitored by the BBC. He continued:

> T'Archbishop of Canterbury orders prayers for Bolshevism. English politicians acquit Soviet Russia of accusations of Atheism. But the historical truth shows that Bolshevism knows neither religion nor nationality. Stalin walks in blood over humanity, civilization, democracy and Christianity. His system is, and always will be, a system of Bolshevik mass butchery. The bloodshed of Jewish Bolshevism united with Jewish plutocracy should be a warning to us. We must close our ranks and not rest till Communism is overcome.

In late '45, Chappel was picked up in Berlin—ironically at a flat across the road from the new Naafi—after accusations of treachery from his fellow POWs were made known to the intelligence services.

He was transported to the British military prison in Brussels, where during interrogations, he argued, in the hope of receiving a lighter sentence, that he was 'never a soldier, but a Naafi worker, under civilian contract.' Chappel also maintained that he was a lifelong socialist and anti-fascist, but his shameful background as a supporter of the Mosley fascist movement was unearthed. At a court-martial, he was slapped with a 15-year prison sentence – enough time for resentment and regret.

CHAPTER 17
WIVES ARRIVE

DURING the first year of the Allied occupation of Germany, Naafi had been catering exclusively to military personnel, but in the spring of 1946, as a result of an extraordinary predicament, this arrangement saw a drastic change.

The War Office was aware that separation was having a negative impact on married troops, and began to seek properties to use as quarters for couples.

Back home, wives struggling with single motherhood also made their voices heard.

The eventual solution was *Operation Union-* allowing any man who had spent one year in Germany (with another year of service ahead of him) to apply to have his family join him on the continent. Not surprisingly, the scheme was a popular: census figures show that 2,038 officers and 3,246 soldiers of other ranks applied to the programme.

When the move finally happened, a journalist with the *Yorkshire Post and Leeds Intelligencer* described the 'the jolliest invasion army embarkation officers have ever had to organise.'

> So important did the BAOR authorities consider this first major invasion under 'Operation Union' that the Rhine Army Commander, General Sir Richard McCreery made a special 250-mile flight last night from his headquarters to Cuxhaven to meet the 552 wives and children forming the first party. It was magnificent North Sea morning

when the Anchor liner *Empire Halladale*, the former German South American service steamer, berthed at Cuxhaven to music from the joint bands the East Lanes and Essex Regiments playing from the bandstand the pier.[109]

However, the situation presented a profound challenge, and, in the rush to get ready, some homes were forcibly requisitioned from German families—a step that caused unease among some members of the British community. Somewhat paradoxically, Prime Minister Clement Attlee warned women joining their husbands that they would be 'looked on by Germans as representatives of the British Empire and that on their behaviour and that of their children, far more than that of the armed forces, the Germans will judge the British and the British way of life.'

The arrival of the first dependents on August 29th, 1946, caught Naafi frantically preparing to open 'Family Shops.'

After some chaos and paper shuffling, copious supplies of nappies, perfumes, baking goods, ornaments, and ladies periodicals were dispatched. Of course, there were some hiccups in the supply chain, and whilst staples like bread, potatoes, milk, meat, and sausage were usually available, there seemed to be a continual shortage of women's clothing and haberdashery.

Clothing coupons were issued to families, although at first, only children's clothes and footwear was obtainable from the Naafi shops. The ration for families included 21lb, 3oz. of meat, 4oz of cheese, 4lb, 6oz. of bread, 14oz

---

[109] Yorkshire Post and Leeds Intelligencer, Monday 2nd September, 1946.

of sugar and 2oz of butter. Additional food, which like in the UK was provided on points, was available from Naafi. British wives were annoyed at not being allowed supplement their basic rations with locally sourced fish, fruit and vegetables, as it was is illegal to buy on the German economy.

Dissatisfaction arose over other matters—in particular regarding the quality and presentation of Naafi products, which forces wives compared unfavourably to their UK counterparts.

No advertising existed in print or radio. Any special offers—usually perishables on the verge of expiration—would be stacked next to the till in the Family Stores. Nevertheless, due in no small part to the circumstances of temporary expatriation, demand remained high, and the tail end of 1946 saw even more customers queuing to use Naafi after a sudden onrush of other arrivals touched-down.

Communities of Servicemen and their families grew to include civilian administrators, along with health care and education services. A team of qualified midwives set up clinics and small maternity wards, followed by 300 teachers for new schools serving forces children. Another huge customer base came from the vast *Control Commission*, a largely civilian body in the British zone, which had the task of directing the shattered nation into the economic shape and giving people accustomed totalitarianism 'a spiritual rebirth and education' in the ways democracy and decent living.' The Commission impinged on practically every form human endeavour. Within a year, the *British Army of the Rhine* had mushroomed into a vast organisation, employing, in addition to military personnel, logistic, administrative, education, construction and welfare professionals.

Its unsurprising then that Naafi became a crucial community focal point. But, despite its importance, the government considered that the school fees in respect of the children of Naafi employees in Germany should not be borne by Army Funds, meaning a compulsory charge of £23 per child per term was payable – it was an issue which angered many Naafi employees.

Although Germany provided a form of escape from the privations of post-war Britain, many families soon discovered it was not the utopia they had expected. Before heading to Germany, wives had received a welter of pamphlets advising them about conditions in the former *Third Reich*. A common complaint—conspicuously unaddressed in these pamphlets—had to do with boredom: once ensconced in their new quarters, forces wives found that they had plenty of free time but little with which to fill it.

The daily routine of seeing the same people and visiting the same clubs could be exasperating. Furthermore, living in a battered and wrecked country, with no amenities or attractions other than those found on the garrison, could be difficult. It was not uncommon for dependents to succumb to depression.

Dorothy Kennedy paid a disastrous eight-week visit to her husband in the British Zone in late 1946, where she witnessed starving German children foraging in dustbins for something to eat. 'Somehow, I felt I could not hate the Germans anymore,' she said. 'Other wives felt like that.' Kennedy also rejected the 'fancy newspaper stories' about military families in Germany eating hams, turkeys and eggs as fabrications: 'We had only army rations,' she said, 'and when the bread ran out we had to eat army biscuits.'

For some, booze made life in the British Zone bearable. Unlike other luxuries, liquor was not in short supply: as Naafi produced over 200,000 bottles of gin every month, along with other spirits and beers, making it cheap and widely available.

Many forces wives managed to develop a lucrative sideline selling Naafi goods on the black market. In their own defence, they blamed the high cost of living .

There was always a ready cash-market for lipstick, powder, soap, coffee, and spirits. 'Black-marketing makes us ashamed but we have no choice. Unlike *Foreign Office* people, we get no overseas allowances,' one wife told the *Daily Express.*

Another spouse in Berlin explained how the black market operated:

> Many of us share a charwoman or make German friends. We sell tea, coffee, and drinks through them at slightly lower prices than they would pay in German shops. Naafi prices are higher than in England, but German shop prices are still higher.

In fact, there was a huge difference in prices. For adults, Naafi rationed gin at two bottles a month and whisky at one bottle a month. But brandy, rum, and wine were free for all. Profit on a bottle of rum: 12 marks (£1) and whisky: 20 marks (£1.14s.).

Another army wife said that with black market profits she could get hold of German shoes and clothing. 'Prices are higher, quality lower, but at least there is more variety than in Naafi, and no five-week wait as with shopping by post.'

Of the rations, all wives agreed that: 'They are

disgraceful. Half the meat is bone, and meat and vegetables are second quality.'

Army life could be difficult for some new arrivals. Living in quarters furnished identically to those of your neighbour (everyone was provided with the same government-issued beds, curtains, cutlery, and so on) could irritating. Some thrived in the new communities and embraced regimental life, but for others, it was too burdensome and many marriages ended with wives packing up and returning to Britain.

In the first phase of *Operation Union*, records show that just over 3,200 Army families went out to Germany. Of those, 18 families returned, and 12 more applied to do so soon after.

***

The year 1948 marked a turning point for post-war Germany with the introduction of the new *Deutsche Mark* in the West, putting the country on the path to normality. Almost immediately, cigarettes and chocolate ceased to the de facto currency, slowing the illicit trade in Naafi goods.

United States aid under the *Marshall Plan* helped kick-start an economic revival in the West along capitalist lines, many US politicians approved the aid because they feared Communism, not because they wanted U.S. dollars to rehabilitate the shaken Germany economy.

But, it was the new monetary reforms which lead to one of the first major international crises of the Cold War. Russia, irked by the new currency, adopted their own 'East Mark' in their areas of occupation.[110]

---

[110] Creation of an economically stable western Germany required reform of the old Reichsmark. The Soviets had debased the Reichsmark by

As relations rapidly chilled, old British ideas about keeping Germans at arm's length dissolved as new alignments developed. Montgomery's fraternisation diktats were discarded and friendships with Germans became not only permitted, but positively encouraged.

The immediate beneficiaries was not only lonely British soldiers. The Naafi wasted no time in hiring young frauleins at much lower wages than their British counterparts at canteens, shops and stores across the British zone.

By March 1948, the Russians began using the introduction of the reformed currency in the West as an excuse for blockading Berlin.

It started with delaying American trains heading into the capital through eastern Germany by demanding impromptu passenger checks or falsely citing incorrect documentation. Soon after, British trains were targeted, followed by obstructions to traffic on the city waterways. By late June the autobahn, rail, and water traffic servicing the Western sectors of Berlin became strangled and ground to a halt.

The Berlin blockade hit the population of the West hard, as limited coal resources meant only hospitals could be heated, and an immediate tightening of rations was introduced.

For normality to be restored, the Russians demanded western powers scrap the new *Deutsche Mark*, but Washington and London brushed off the request and responded with an airlift campaign to bypass the blocked roads, rail and waterways.

The operation to carry supplies to the people of West

---

excessive printing, resulting in Germans using cigarettes as a de facto currency or for bartering. The Soviets opposed western plans for a reform. They interpreted this new currency as an unjustified, unilateral decision.

Berlin was enormous. Pilots from the Royal Air Force, US Air Force, French Air Force, the Royal Canadian Air Force, the Royal Australian Air Force, the Royal New Zealand Air Force, and the South African Air Force flew over 200,000 supply flights in one year, keeping Berliners fed and stocked with fuel.[111]

The Soviets, fearing the possibility of open conflict, did not disrupt the airlift. Soon after the blockade began, British families and messes in Berlin had their coal and coke supplies cut by half, and a strict watch was kept on their petrol consumption. Bars were shut early, and supplementary foodstuffs through the Naafi were restricted.

RAF Gatow in West Berlin was earmarked as an airlift depot, as German civilian construction workers rushed to lay a third runway to cope with the heavy traffic.

Mr. McGarrell, who was the charge hand of the Naafi grocery stores in Berlin, lived in a tent on the airfield day and night; making sure the two-full aircraft loads of supplies arriving daily was dispatched correctly.

Mr McGarrell would have kept a close eye on the movement of booze and luxury goods, which occasionally turned out to be a thorny issue during the blockade. On one occasion, several dozen cases of Scotch whisky destined for Gatow on an RAF Dakota, were guarded by a Naafi controller to ensure they did not go astray when the plane landed. And in another incident, the American crew of a C54 became so angry when they discovered their cargo was wine for the sole use of French soldiers, that they refused to take-off, contending milk deliveries were more important.

---

[111] American traffic flew to and from Tempelhof Airport by a southern corridor, by the central corridor traffic flew between Wunstorf and Gatow; by the northern corridor Dakota traffic flies between Fassberg and Gatow.

Then there was the time the British commandant in Berlin ordered more 'luxury' items to be shipped in for Naafi, as he considered the French and Americans were being offered much better goods by their respective canteens.[112]

In addition to the Naafi's regular duties, the task of serving aircrews, builders and the thousands of drivers and labours working round-the-clock became a priority. Mobile canteens were stationed outside hangers and beside runways. The Gatow Naafi club continuously served hot food, and even laid-on tea for Prime Minister Clement Attlee when he arrived to meet young serviceman on the base. Electricity cuts were common, with working under the glow of oil lamps becoming a regular occurrence. In fact, the coal shortage meant that hospitals, telephone exchanges, newspapers, and other essential non-industrial undertakings were supplied with their own electric generators.

At Wunsdorf, near Hannover, Naafi workers toiled day and night loading relief aircraft – as well as supplying a 24-hour canteen service. The Naafi in-house journal noted:

> Naafi women mobile canteen drivers and their assistants are doing sterling work in the round-the-clock service for the airlift at Wunsdorf. One of them is ex-dressmaker Mrs. D. Hearn of East Croydon, who during the war changed her sewing machine for a civil defence ambulance. Another is Mrs. D. Banks of Horley, who before joining Naafi, drove for three and a half years in the WAAF.[113]

---

[112] The Blockade Breakers by Helena P. Schrader. The History Press.

[113] 'Operation Plain Fair', *Naafi News*, Winter 1947

RAF Fassberg in Lower Saxony also played an important role as a hub for supplying Berlin. It was there, behind the wheel of a mobile canteen, that Miss Clarice Collis-Bird could be found darting around the airstrip from daybreak till sunset. She had joined Naafi in 1944, after serving as the personal driver of Clement Atlee for five-years, where she 'delivered him to innumerable wartime engagements.'

By the spring of 1949, it was clear that the airlift was succeeding, and by April – at the same time Nato was formed - it was delivering more cargo than had previously been transported into the city by rail.[114]

General Herbert, the British Commander in Berlin remarked: 'We are in a strong position for food, stocks of rations and Naafi supplies are higher than they were before the blockade started.'

After a year, Russia gave up and restored the rail link between West Germany and West Berlin – but there was no relaxation of strained relations between the Allies and USSR.

According to legend, probably dreamt in the Naafi PR department, the first Allied vehicle to re-enter the city post-blockade was none other than a mobile canteen.

Soon, plentiful supplies of food began to arrive and normality was gradually restored.

Anyone that knows Germany will be aware of a local delicacy known as the 'bratwurst'. Despite being popular with Germans, these huge sausages were often given a wide berth by British soldiers, as their ingredients of

---

[114] The North Atlantic Treaty Organisation (Nato) was formed by the United States, Canada and ten European states on April 4th, 1949 in Washington, D.C.

blood, brains, liver and bacon thrust into bladder or intestine was hard to stomach.

However, in September 1949, Herta Heuwer changed all that after setting up a tiny wooden kiosk across the road from the Charlottenburg railway station in the British Zone. From there, she began dishing out an unusual dish for 60 pfennigs a portion.

Herta Heuwer

Her sole pre-war occupation had been as a shop assistant, and her story is similar to that of Tesco's Jack Cohen, in as much as she also carved out a successful career thanks to Naafi.

Somehow - probably through the black market – Herta managed to obtain bottles of tomato ketchup, Worcestershire sauce and curry powder from the Naafi shop. She then mixed the ingredients together and poured it over grilled sausages – giving birth to the Currywurst. Even though Frankfurter sausages, are still eaten by everybody, the once popular Blutwurst, Mettwurst and Leberwurst cannot compete with her curried sausage.

Herta patented her recipe in the 50s, and although she did not earn millions, she bought a nice house and enjoyed a comfortable retirement until her death in 1999.[115]

---

[115] As of 2018, it was estimated that 800 million currywursts are eaten every year in Germany.

CHAPTER 18
KOREA

THE 1950s saw the beginning of the end of drab post-war life. Bewildered pensioners heard *Rock 'n' Roll* for the first time, television started beaming into homes across the country, the Coronation captivated the nation and austerity gradually gave way to consumerism – triggering a monumental change in the way people shopped.

Naafi remained a giant retail and catering concern. It was active in Aden, Athens, Asmara, Benghazi, Derna, Freetown, Gibraltar, Hong Kong, Kuala Lumpur, Mombassa, Nairobi, Nicosia, Port Said, Salonika, Singapore, Suez, Tobruk, Tripoli, Trieste and Vienna. In Britain, clubs serviced garrisons at Aldershot, Bicester, Carlisle, Catterick Camp, Chatham, Chester, Colchester, Darlington, Lincoln, Manchester, Nottingham, Oswestry, Plymouth, Portsmouth, Salisbury and Southampton.

At Denbury, counter-girl Eve Diett remembered the Naafi became the preferred hangout for bored National Servicemen, with the morning tea break - when soldiers fell into line at the counter - being a particularly testing time.

> There'd be a long queue, which would often trail off outside, and I always wanted to get them served as quick as I could. Sometimes they used to mess around in the queue – especially if you had one or two that were a bit 'slow on the uptake.' I used to scream, if you don't hurry up, I'm going to pull the shutters down. The sergeant

major sometime used to come in and shout - he used to scare me.'

These same servicemen were well aware that trouble had been brewing in North-East Asia. Tensions had been escalating for some time, prompting communist North Korea to invade its neighbour and kindred spirit, South Korea. The United Nations, the United States and many other countries, rallied to the defence of the South. China, unsurprisingly, mobilized in support of its political compatriots on the northern half of the peninsula.

Soon after, Great Britain announced that it was sending elements of its *Far East Fleet* to the Korean coast, together with ships of Commonwealth navies.

Although soldiers usually hide their fears - often from each other - Eve remembers many were terrified and afraid of what might happen.

> They were only young, they were about 18 or 19 - they were fresh-faced and were absolutely scared stiff and were drilled really hard. They had never experienced anything like that before. Some of them committed suicide, while I was there. I used to watch them being drilled on the parade ground, and the sergeant major was a nasty bit of work. One shot himself in the foot so he couldn't go to Korea, then another one 'accidentally' electrocuted himself when he was pressing his trousers – standing in a pool of water – he died. Another one shot himself in the ablutions.

Naafi also prepared for action, as 45 personnel were sent to the fleet, serving in the Naval Canteen Service. British battalions from Hong Kong, the Middlesex and the Argyll and Sutherland Highlanders, and an Australian battalion from Japan joined the action.

Naafi tea was a popular commodity in Korea.

Naafi needed more men and called for 200 volunteers - half of whom were to be posted to Korea and the remainder to be held in reserve.

The ideal candidates were to be ex-servicemen – under 40-years of age - and medically fit to enlist for 18 months service.

In all, 100 ex-servicemen, Naafi staff and former members of the EFI made the journey out to Korea, landing in Pusan on November 21st, 1950.

They soon found that supplying such a large army no easy task, especially when faced with appalling weather, logistical nightmares and a lack of adequate sanitation. Soon after landing, Naafi canteens were chugging down rutted Korean roads, amid a conflict that would eventually draw in 100,000 British service personnel.

'We suddenly got word that a Naafi truck was appearing on the scene,' Ralph Horsfield of the 1st Bn Argyll and Sutherland Highlanders recalled of his first experience of seeing the institute in Korea. 'At that time they were selling things like packets of good old Blighty tea and sugar…our purchases weren't things like chocolate, I don't think they sold that, it was purely tea, sugar and tins of milk.'

EFI corporal, C. Spragg, wrote home: 'A great drawback here is the water, which we must not use either for drinking or washing unless it has been treated . . . we have gone dirty for two days. . . . At our last stop, we managed to cook a bit of breakfast over two small tins filled with petrol. When we stop people seem to come from nowhere and there are thousands of children begging, but we dare not give them anything or the entire population would soon be around us.'

The weather in Korea is unpredictable and can change quickly from tropical to almost Arctic. For three years, Naafi drivers navigated roads that were nothing more than dirt tracks. On one occasion, Chinese Communist prisoners of war, tired and haggard, sat down with their captors hoping to draw some succour from a refreshing cup of tea at the *Newcastle Corner House*, an EFI canteen near the front.

Spragg also noted the difficulty in making deliveries: 'This is our eighth day and we have just delivered supplies to the troops. Everybody was waiting for them as they had run out of cigarettes. You can guess we were very welcome. We shall be on that dreadful journey back tonight, but are hoping to get a bath and some clean clothes when we reach our base.'

Even faced with such horrendous conditions, Naafi was singled out for high praise from the British Commander of the Commonwealth base, who remarked: 'No complaints of shortage of supplies. Mobile canteens are working in Brigade areas and doing a brisk trade. Staff remained cheerful, willing and hard-working under most trying conditions.'

In May 1953, correspondent John Walters stopped by a Naafi store in Korea, which by then had grown substantially in size and service.

'Frankly, I'm surprised by the transparent negligee that the Naafi now sells to our men,' he reported. 'It was funny to hear Tommies and NCOs arguing whether or not such flimsily daring gifts would please their wives and sweethearts at home.' Walters didn't dare to speculate whether the items would indeed help to spice up a relationship gone stale, but did add: 'A sergeant-major told me that when he sent his wife in Lancashire a transparent pink negligee he received a suspicious reproof instead of gratitude.' 'Alf,' she wrote, 'I can't possibly wear that kind of thing in Bolton. Korea seems to be giving you strange ideas of what's proper.'

As it turned out, the only British civilians to have seen action in the Korean War were volunteer canteen staff on board Royal Navy ships. Five of those volunteers served on *HMS Jamaica* when she was hit by a shell from a shore battery. Margaret Holt – the only British female sent to the country - spent a year teaching the locals to cook for the *Commonwealth Division*. On her return to London, she said Koreans thought the staple meal in the UK was egg, beans and chips. 'The most difficult job I had was to teach them to make tea from boiling water.'

Naafi employee James Tait, a Scot in charge of the first mobile canteen to follow assault troops across the Imjin and Han Rivers, wrote a book on his experiences in Korea —which was read by President Eisenhower. Tait collected the material for his story – *The American Soldier* - whilst serving with Naafi from December 1950, until February 1952.

During the *Second World War* he was with the Royal Artillery in Iceland, Burma and India, and after his demobilisation, found work in Switzerland, before volunteering for service with Naafi in Korea.

Tait said that one of his happier tasks was to escort stars who came out to entertain the troops, and recalled meetings with Danny Kaye, Jack Warner and Ethel Revnell. While he was in Korea he received letters from King George VI and Prime Minister Attlee, congratulating him the work he was doing there. His book did briefly mention Naafi:

> Because of transportation costs, Naafi prices are high to the British troops, but if they had as many free issues as the Americans, there would be no need for Naafi in Korea.

Tait was right. The fact that Naafi charges for shaving and tooth brushes and cleaning equipment were higher in other areas, particularly Germany, caused widespread grumbling.

To calm frayed tempers, Naafi 'pushed the boat out' for the Christmas celebrations in 1953. Decorations were despatched to Korea and hung in the three Naafi roadhouses strategically sited on the military road feeding the forward areas. 'There are no shortages and everything possible is being done to ensure that British soldiers out there will be able to celebrate Christmas Day in the traditional manner,' a Naafi spokesman said. The roadhouses were unique structures, fashioned from timber and built to Naafi specifications. Their construction was documented by EFI member Frank Soden, who observed that when the operation started it was 'the most talked about project in Korea that resulted in rebuilt roadhouses in picturesque old-world pub style with timbered ceilings, thatched roofs (rice straw from paddy fields), brick and tiled fireplaces - a welcome change from the smelly oil stoves that heated the tents - gaily painted window frames and doors. The buildings were surrounded by vehicle parks and gardens, where during the summer, brightly coloured umbrellas stood among the seats and tables.'

One of the few existing photos of a Naafi 'roadhouse' in Korea, slightly out of focus due to an early colouring process.

The conflict eventually became bogged down into a battle of attrition –cutting short the lives of 1,000 British, as well as over 48,000 American soldiers. Millions of

Koreans and Chinese died in the conflict, of which the fighting ended with a shaky peace deal in 1953 although the two countries are technically still at war to this day.

The final chapter in the Korean conflict saw a former Naafi club at Southampton being turned into a hotel to house relatives of 580 ex-Korean prisoners of war who arrived home in September 1953. The British Red Cross Society provided mattresses, blankets and pillows, whilst cutlery and other equipment was supplied the Naafi.

***

At the height of the Korean adventure, the British government had also been focused on other issues, in particular, the growing influence of atomic weaponry.

In mid-1952, fifteen Naafi workers witnessed Britain enter the nuclear age when they accompanied troops and scientists to Montebello Islands, off the coast of north-western Australia. Here, the first-ever atomic weapon test by the United Kingdom took place on October 3rd, 1952. Gilbert Vine, the manager of the Naafi canteen in Monte Bello, witnessed this earth-shattering event – which elevated Britain to become the third nuclear power.

Nearby, William Penney, the scientific director, noted how everybody watched in silence as a terrifying – a great greyish cloud was hurled thousands of feet into the air and 'increasing in size with astonishing rapidity'. Once newspapers had exhausted every angle of the story, William Vine, stepped forward with a Naafi angle, which involved a charismatic five-foot lizard.

'I had to set up shop at first in a tent on an island that looked as though it had already been hit by an atom bomb,' Vine explained, adding that *Charley Boy* made his home in the canteen and earned his keep.

There was hardly any vegetation—just sand—and animal life was confined to rats, measuring up to 16 inches from nose to tail tip. Luckily, *Charley Boy* took care of the rat problem. The iguanas lived on the rats and the rats tried to live on us

Another headache was the 'millions of flies', including a particularly peculiar brand that had spurs on their legs.

The island's annual rainfall was eight inches, which Vine added, fell in the first week and washed away the Naafi marquee. Thankfully, the posting was over by December, and the *HMS Campania* returned everyone home in time for Christmas.

CHAPTER 19
SUEZ CRISIS

DESPITE her nuclear prowess, London was presiding over an Empire on the wane. The dying days of Britain's colonial interest in Egypt began in 1951, in the wake of rising nationalism and the abolition of a long-standing treaty between Cairo and London. The opening shot in this souring relationship occurred at a Naafi.

Troops guard the burned out Naafi stores in Ismailia

The tense situation exploded on October 16th, when Egyptians stormed the Naafi stores in Ismailia, stabbing a British soldier. From the veranda of her flat, a young British woman witnessed the scene: 'We heard shouts and then saw smoke pouring from the Naafi. Egyptian civilians started looting and then to fight among themselves for the possession the loot.'[116]

The situation escalated quickly. Egyptians employees of Naafi – totalling 4,000 workers – downed tools and quit their jobs. Naafi continued to be caught up as the violence spread. A Naafi truck with two native employees was ambushed on the desert road wounding the driver, and then a few weeks later, armed terrorists fired two bursts at a Naafi car near Ismailia.

In November, Egyptian terrorists gagged and bound to a chair the wife of a Naafi official in her home. They searched every room in the house, but left without taking anything. In a desperate attempt to calm the situation and secure Britain's economic and strategic interests – troops began arriving en masse from the UK.

In response, Egyptian volunteers rushed to join the anti-British fight, with the *Muslim Brotherhood* in Ismailia declaring a jihad. The tensions led to the declaration of an emergency period.

To ensure that Naafi could service the 85,000 British troops in the Canal Zone, 600 extra staff were flown in from London. But the strain for both troops and Naafi workers could be intense.

In February 1952, a British Army captain and a corporal were shot dead and a private wounded by a burst of gunfire at a party for all ranks at a Naafi canteen in Suez, a RASC corporal was arrested.

To relieve the obvious pressures of working in such a powder keg, some servicemen and women deployed in

---

[116] Account of Isa Patterson. Until the riots started, Mrs Patterson and her children lived in civilian flats at Ismailia. *Dundee Courier* December 8th, 1951.

Suez were given breaks at Naafi's *Golden Sands* holiday camp near Famagusta on the shores of Cyprus, where guests could enjoy dining with waiter service, an old English style tavern and various lounges.

A separate Alpine styled Naafi camp called *Pine Tree* offered the simple outdoors life high up on Mount Olympus. Between May and October 1954, 16,500 servicemen from Suez spent from one to four weeks on the island, arriving aboard specially chartered aircraft to Nicosia.

The emergency lasted until 1954 when the UK pulled-out. But it was not the end of the matter.

In late 1956, the British and French-owned canal was nationalised by the President Gamal Abdel Nasser, the charismatic young President – and a champion of pan-Arab nationalism. The waterway was the lifeline to the British in the Far East and India and gave easy access to vast supplies of British owned oil in Iran and Iraq. It is estimated that a quarter of imports to the United Kingdom and a third of its shipping sailed through it.

On November 5th, a British – French force of paratroopers landed on the banks of the canal, as RAF jets bombed Cairo, aiming to regain Western control of the canal and to remove Nasser.

An EFI contingent of 100 men stood by in Cyprus to support the operation, having been given training, issued with Sten guns and inoculated. The crisis, like so many others, showed that Naafi had nearly perfected cobbling together a service, even in the most extreme circumstances. Prior to the paratroopers leaving for Suez, Naafi in Akrotiri kept French contingent fed a staple diet of meat pies and rock-cakes – washed down with a surprising amount of local wine.

Four EFI officers, along with eighteen men, followed on

the heels of British troops into Port Said, operating a canteen and bulk stores.[117] But the effort was short lived. After the fighting had started, political pressure from the United States, the Soviet Union, and the United Nations led to a withdrawal by the invaders.

The episode succeeded in humiliating Great Britain and France and strengthened Nasser.

Accused of 'gunboat diplomacy,' the embattled Prime Minister Anthony Eden resigned, leaving British prestige in tatters.

---

[117] *Service to the Services* by Harry Miller. Page 98. Miller adds that Naafi efforts in Suez during 1956 earned the commendation of the DA and QMG Brigadier JHS Lacey. He noted "The unit has worked itself into the ground and produced a Naafi service, which during the planning days in London, we never thought possible".

CHAPTER 20
CYPRUS

CYPRUS was considered a plum posting, especially for those packed off with their families to seaside garrisons - a world away from the austerity of post-war Britain.

The Mediterranean island was an area of vital strategic importance, as troops based there could be switched quickly to any Middle East or Gulf trouble spot at a moment's notice.

Regulars reminisce that the early 1950s were halcyon days. Cyprus provided a good standard of living, reasonably high wages, and benefits such as modern healthcare. Many National Service conscripts, however, had contrasting fortunes, complaining that their tour of duty could be a miserable experience billeted in camps built around eight-foot tents and wooden huts.

In late 1954, Cyprus acquired a new significance after the evacuation of British troops from the Suez Canal Zone, as noted in the previous chapter.

Soon after, the island became a hive of military activity as work began on a £10 million project to transform the Dhekelia garrison into a 'Mediterranean Aldershot' with three hundred new married quarters, a high street - boasting a cinema, bank, post office, church – and a Naafi department store. 'This is the soldier's dream home—and paradise,' was the verdict of the British press.

The chief planner, Lieutenant Colonel C.E Wrath, crowed that the garrison would not 'look, sound or even smell-like any other army camp.' Warth's plan was to develop a 'civvy street' atmosphere, akin to the, at the time, massively popular seaside towns in the United Kingdom. 'Dhekelia will keep them in the army alright,' he boasted.

Naafi in Cyprus benefited from deals with local breweries including Keo and Leon, along with wine producers, farmers and butchers.

They bought and exported oranges, the famed *Commandaria* wine and red-soil Cyprus potatoes to other branches in the Mediterranean, whilst also becoming one of the major employers on the island. Shops and canteens recorded brisk business in Akrotiri, Paphos, and Episkopi on the west coast, up in the Troodos Mountains, and also in Famagusta, Dhekelia, Ayios Nikolaos, and Cape Greco on the east coast.

In all, there were thirty-six canteens, twelve mobile canteens, eleven families' shops, a garrison club for other ranks, one sports shop and three leave centres. In addition, Naafi provided kiosks on some of the bathing beaches.

Suddenly, this plum posting turned sour in April 1955, when the *National Organization of Cypriot Fighters* —known as EOKA—kicked off a rebellion against the British, leaving London stunned and setting in motion a tragic chain of events ultimately resulting in the deaths of 457 British personnel and at least 90 Cypriot fighters.

That spring, the Cypriot fighters began a violent island-wide guerrilla campaign against the British using all the tactics you might expect, including assassinations, ambushes, bombings, and sabotage.

Operating from secret hideouts in the Troodos Mountains, EOKA members were led by the charismatic Greek General George Grivas, known by the pseudonym 'Digenis.'

Far from the peace and tranquillity that they had been

expecting, the 18,000 British troops on Cyprus suddenly faced a terrifying battle for their own survival as casualties mounted. Those families that felt growing alarm at the situation battened down behind the protective barbed wire of camps, whilst some wives and children fled to the safety of the UK.

British troops were no longer able to enjoy Cypriot bars, nightclubs, beaches, shops or taverns - resulting in boredom plaguing the barrack blocks. At one garrison near Nicosia, 800 men were obliged to share a single table tennis set, a handful of chessboards, and one billiard table.

The *Daily Mirror* takes up the plight of soldiers in Cyprus

Few dispute that Naafi canteens in Cyprus were dreary and unlovely. Journalist Denis Martin described them as 'sombre, workhouse looking sort of places.'

The army might reasonably ask the Naafi, which has a virtual monopoly now that the Greek shops are almost all out of bounds, to use its profits to provide billiard tables, table tennis sets and so on...

Martin's report christened Cyprus *Terror Island* and peddled the recurring theme of soldiers complaining. In this case, the simple pleasure of a bottle of beer in the Naafi cost 2 shillings—'more than their overseas allowance for a day.' A few weeks prior, the Secretary of State for War had been asked in the House of Commons 'whether he was aware of the discontent among soldiers serving in Cyprus due to the high charges for essentials and for luxuries in the Naafi.'

'I know the British army well enough to know that it always complains about Naafi prices,' War Minister Antony Head barked back.[118] Serviceman Terry O'Reilly was familiar with the gripers and groaners:

> There were moans about Naafi prices. But compared to what? On the few occasions that we did get off camp and into the towns - Famagusta for us - the prices of goods and drinks seemed a little higher.[119]

O'Reilly's free time was spent at a bleak Naafi set-up at

---

[118] 'Naafi Prices in Cyprus', House of Commons debate. March 27th, 1956. George Thomas MP for Cardiff West asked: "Is the Minister not aware that there has been considerable publicity in the Press to the effect that our troops are dissatisfied over this matter? Head responded: "I also saw the article, which I think was in the *News Chronicle*. It said that a bar of chocolate, which I call a slab, costs 11d., and a bottle of beer 1s., but it omitted to say that it was a quart bottle and that cigarettes cost 1s. for twenty. I admit that certain prices are higher in Cyprus because of local import duties, but the local overseas allowance is worked out to cover those charges.

[119] Terry O'Reilly interview with author Nathan Morley, 2017.

Cape Greco manned by Greek Cypriot men. 'Prices must have been OK,' he recalled, as 'even the poor National Service lads seemed to have their fill. Still, we were all young lads, 18 or 19, some first-time drinkers got kayoed on two pints... the moaners were mostly National Service and many had a jaundiced view of all things service-related.'

John Barry, who later found fame as a composer, spent his National Service at a camp near Larnaca in the east. The huge amount of free time offered him the chance to study music:

> There was nothing to do except go to a local village and get drunk, so I sat in the storehouse with a piano for sixteen months and taught myself arranging.

Barry took up a correspondence course with jazz musician Bill Russo in Chicago, later recalling: 'there was this guy who had one of these shops that sell ashtrays and things with maps on them. I used to go in once a week, with my army pay, buy the dollars, put the cash in an envelope and send them to Bill in Chicago'.

Along with 15 other conscripts, Barry also formed a band that played exclusively at a unique venue—a Naafi hut, where their weekly gigs received a boisterous reception as squaddies grooved 'til the wee hours to the sounds of Glen Miller, Count Basie, and Ted Heath. After leaving the army, Barry famously went on to write scores for Hollywood blockbusters such as *The Ipcress File, Zulu, Midnight Cowboy*, and eleven James Bond films.

By late 1958, the EOKA campaign had ramped up to alarming proportions. In September, a Naafi used by civilians near Limassol was gutted by fire; it was believed the blaze was started by the freedom fighters, who considered Naafi as fair game.

A few weeks later, a bomb blew up on a luggage trolley next to an RAF *Comet* jetliner at Nicosia airport. Thankfully, the plane's departure had been delayed—the bags had not yet been loaded onto the aircraft. The bomb went off just before the *Comet* was due to leave. and while the men were clustered round their luggage near the aircraft waiting for a security check. Ten men were injured in the atrocity, which was blamed on a time bomb hidden in a bottle of wine bought at the Naafi, where Greek Cypriots were employed. John Mossman, the Nicosia reporter of the *Daily Herald* described the scene: 'Alongside the gangway was the pile of hand luggage waiting be searched by security men. Then came the blast. Men were blown from the gangway. Blood stained the runway. Bags and brief cases were blown open. And from one came a trickle of sweet Cyprus wine'.

Soon after that incident , a huge fire broke out the Naafi furniture depot near Famagusta docks after a gang of masked gunmen entered the store and ordered all Cypriot employees out of the building at gunpoint. Then they poured petrol over the furniture and set it alight.

The incidents led to the sacking of all 500 Greek Cypriot Naafi workers. Initially, army wives took their place to keep things running.

Martin Bell, the former BBC correspondent who served in Cyprus at that time, remembers how 'the quality of the cakes and biscuits actually improved.'[120] New helpers came from the UK after a national press campaign appealed for staff to work on the island. Unsurprisingly, with an attractive salary of £8/10/- or eight pounds and

---

[120] Martin Bell interview with author Nathan Morley, 2017.

ten shillings for men and £7/15/- for women, applications flooded in.

Each new worker was also offered £3 a week 'danger money' along with full board. Within a week of the first advertisement being published, 700 people had applied and been interviewed.

The old Naafi at Nicosia airport, now in the UN Buffer Zone. (Photo: Nathan Morley).

A further 7,300 had phoned the Naafi to express interest in joining the organisation. Applicants ranged invocation from typists and shop assistants to factory workers and cinema usherettes.

That inspirational Naafi figurehead Humphrey Prideaux said: 'a complete cross-section of the community' had applied from right across Great Britain: 'The majority have no other motive than to serve our men in Cyprus.' In all, Naafi received 17,000 applications.

Still, the situation was fragile. An editorial, the *Daily Mirror* made several demands:

- **No Naafi women and girls should go out to Cyprus**
- **No more soldiers' families should go out to Cyprus**
- **Those already there should be brought back**

In the Commons, Prime Minister, Harold Macmillan admitted that the situation was so bad that no more dependants of soldiers would be sent to the island. He did, however, acknowledge the 'desire of the troops to have their families with them.'

On November 17th, 1958, the first party of British Naafi volunteers arrived aboard a *Vickers Viscount* airliner. When the 42 men and women touched down, twenty-one-year-old Sally Anne Heath was the first new Naafi member to step onto the tarmac. Reuters reported:

> There were smiles from the British reception committee and officials at the airport as the volunteers entered the airport buildings. Special security arrangements were in force along their route to the Nicosia hotel - where they will have refreshments before being posted to canteens and stores various parts of Cyprus.

'Sunshine! Lovely!' was reportedly the remark of many of those new arrivals. But, on their way to their hotel, they drove through leaflets fluttering in the streets—presumably distributed by an EOKA operative—denouncing the sacking of Cypriot workers.

The new blood and, presumably, some attractive company, came as a huge morale booster to troops. Two 'RAF corporals' stationed at Akrotiri wrote to the *Daily Mirror* to say that they found the overwhelming response to the Naafi appeal for workers 'encouraging' in that is showed 'somebody thinks of us.'

In another letter, an unnamed Lance Corporal asked readers to 'imagine our pride and gratitude when we hear of the enormous number that volunteered.'

The celebrations were to prove short-lived, as worse was to follow. A powerful time bomb exploded at the Naafi at a Royal Artillery camp in Paphos, leaving 17 soldiers seriously wounded.

Despite the tense times, 'the importance of the Naafi was that it was the nearest thing to a home-away-from-home that we had,' says Martin Bell. 'There was even a quiet corner where we could read newspapers, magazines, and cheap novels. At one point, there was the serious threat of a beer shortage, and emergency supplies were flown in from Malta.'

In the end, British troops proved unable to defeat the EOKA uprising and in 1959 an agreement that Cyprus should become a sovereign independent republic, in return for Britain's retention of rights of two bases - one at Akrotiri and the other in Dhekelia - was reached.

In 1961, the Queen and Prince Philip made a brief stop in Akrotiri en route to India where they held a private talk with the new President, Archbishop Makarios.

The *Cyprus Mail* reported that the meeting set the final seal on the restoration of good relations between the two countries. In fact relations between Nicosia and London had improved so much by 1964, that Naafi organised an eight-day 'Cyprus Festival' which ran concurrently at all Naafi shops in Cyprus and overseas. All kinds of Cypriot products were on display, such as clothing, pottery, fresh fruit, canned products, wines, spirits and beer. The object was to stimulate interest in local produce, with the wine stalls having been 'particularly popular.' Even President Makarios took a personal interest and visited the main Naafi families shop in Nicosia, and expressed pleasure at the display and complimented Naafi for their effort.

Peace was short-lived in the new Republic. Just over a decade later, after the Turkish invasion of the island - which resulted in the occupation of the northern third - an agreement was hammered out by British, Turkish and Greek officers in the old Naafi hut at Nicosia airport on August 9th, 1974.

Afterward, a Turkish colonel 'shook hands hesitantly' with a Greek major. That handshake in the Naafi opened the way for the United Nations to open a buffer-zone and arrange the exchange of prisoners.

CHAPTER 21
MODERNISATION

THE FIFTIES saw Naafi redefine itself, as they upped sticks from their base at Bad Salzuflen and moved southwest of Mönchengladbach to the new headquarters for British forces in Germany. A vast swathe of countryside at Rheindahlen was developed into a largely self-contained community for 8,000 members of the British Rhine Army, RAF and Nato. Known as JHQ, it was the most ambitious building project ever carried out by the War Office.

A grand block - known as 'The Big House' with 2,000 offices - formed its epicentre, with married quarters, schools, churches, cinemas, a swimming pool, Naafi, messes and clubs completing its surroundings.

Anybody that served at JHQ will remember the campus-like appearance with perfectly trimmed lawns and modern buildings. As an administrative and control centre, most people worked normal civilian hours and British families mingled with Dutch, German, French, Belgian, American and Canadian Servicemen.

In the early days, one sergeant-major, a Scotsman, sourly observed, 'it's more like a holiday camp than an army headquarters,' – and he was right. At nightfall, uniforms disappeared as men and women set off for evening entertainment in a free and easy atmosphere any holiday camp would have been proud of. Entertainment was cheap at the garrison theatre, cinemas and Naafi club, where a half-pint of beer from Holland cost just 6d and latest pop music had customers shaking to the newest craze.

Around this time, Naafi decided to embark on a programme of makeovers at their scruffy counter service branches as the supermarket revolution swept the UK. For the first time, customers were able to touch and inspect items in clean, hygienic and bright surroundings.[121]

Despite the troubles, the airmen of RAF Kabrit in the Suez Zone of Egypt were the unwitting guinea pigs at the first Naafi self-service outlet in 1953, then, another opened at the Allied Air Forces headquarters in Fontainbleau soon after.

That same year, Lancelot Royle retired, his last duty was to open Naafi's own staff training centre at a former Catholic convent called *Totteridge Lodge* on the northern outskirts of London. The facility was described as a 'finishing school for Naafi girls.'

New employees underwent a week's intensive training before being posted to a Service canteen. Within the first 12-months of opening, over 2,000 people had passed through its doors. Naafi historian Harry Miller later noted: 'Cooks had a model kitchen equipped with every kind of stove they were likely to find in a Naafi canteen. Senior people went there for refresher courses but also to have practical experience of the work of their subordinates. Staff going overseas were briefed on the country and its currency.' German members of staff - mostly female counter girls - also attended a month's

---

[121] A few self service stores had started to appear in Britain during the mid 1930s, but their development was cut short by the war. In November 1937, the *Derry Journal* reported that Craig's Self-Service Stores an "entirely new idea in the grocery, provisions, and confectionery lines" had opened in Derry offering "a large selection of goods at competitive prices are on view, all labelled and priced and attractively set out on the shelves for customers to walk in and inspect."

course at the centre.

Meanwhile, back in Germany, the weekly sales of tea and coffee were rationed to 'reasonable amounts' because Naafi, having imported vast quantities of Nescafe into BAOR shops free of duty, were under obligation to prevent their 'misuse' by sale or barter. The Naafi price of coffee was 7s. per lb. and the local price in Germany was 20s. 'That is the situation. If I allowed unlimited supplies of coffee to go it would be asking a lot of housewives and others not to sell it to the Germans,' Anthony Head, Secretary of State for War told parliament.[122] It was not just coffee that raised eyebrows at that time. In 1953 authorities attempted a crack-down on 'obscene' pulp literature, targeting the books of Hank Janson. Copies of "Accused," "Persian Pride," "Amok," "Vengeance," "Killer," "Pursuit and Auction" purchased in bulk by Naafi were quietly withdrawn from shelves. These thrillers, sold in paperback, featured erotic cover art and racy storylines.

The abolition of rationing in 1953 had heralded in a wider range of products becoming available. The look of Naafi shops also improved – with long, soldier-straight rows of shelves, a central island and a till near the door. Over 15,000 different items were being stocked in the larger stores – most of which was lugged to the four corners of the world from the UK.

One of the key objectives was to diversify into new markets. Television sets, washing machines, LP records, shoes and sporting equipment were all given their own space, whilst dividend stamps were introduced at tills as an alternative to discounts.

---

[122] HC Deb 14 April 1953 vol 514 cc20-1

In 1961 alone, Servicemen in Germany bought more than 1,000 cars from the Naafi on *Higher Purchase* (HP), which offered 'favourable' terms to obtain loans for most British and Continental cars. The terms were 20 percent deposit and repayment over three years, with 6 percent interest on the original loan. In some cases, when customers could not meet HP payments, Naafi contacted commanding officers and installments were docked from pay-packets –a situation which caused resentment among troops, angry that Naafi could call in army discipline in such a way.

That same year, a glossy 128-page catalogue was published offering a bewildering variety of items ranging from typewriters, electric shavers, and cameras to spin-dryers and garden swings. Reporter John Baker visited Naafi's 'gigantic modernistic' warehouse in Germany, where staff adapted to supplying the new chain of self-service stores. The complex at Krefeld handled a throughput of 1,000 tons per week.[123]

> Today there are fur coats for others ranks' wives, and motor cars (in Germany. mostly), bicycles, outboard motors, washing machines, spin dryers, refrigerators, cameras, civilian suits and children's clothing, sports equipment from go-karts to curling stones, artificial flowers and thousands of other lines.[124]

---

[123] The 1959 annual turnover was £56million and by 1960 there were 24.000 workers, in 2,000 establishments ranging from plush clubs to one-man stores on navy ships. Naafi was represented in Germany, France. Belgium. Holland. Poland. Hungary, Czechoslovakia, Gibraltar, Malta, Cyprus, Libya, Bahrain, Aden, Kenya, South Africa, Singapore, Malaya, Hong Kong, Jamaica, Ceylon, British Honduras, Guiana, Christmas Island, and on the high seas and even in the Antarctic on research vessels.
[124] Coventry Evening Telegraph - Tuesday 30 August, 1960

Sir William Beale, the black-moustached ex-colonel and chairman of Naafi's board of management, took two minutes to brief Baker on the upgrades, saying, 'Naafi has in effect joined the nuclear age.'

> The fifties saw the end of the 'char and wad' mentality. The old bob-a-day soldier has faded away and Naafi must meet the need of the new-style Serviceman. Naafi is now beginning a new epoch rather than a new decade in a spirit of adventurous experiment.

Beale later observed that there was 'no such thing as a normal Naafi year.' Sir William Beale observed that: 'Normality implies usual and familiar, whereas in Naafi it is always the unusual and unfamiliar which compose the pattern of its trade. In ordinary civilian business - and I write with experience of the distributive trades - some measure of normality, some common factor between one trading period and another may, and indeed must be found if forward plans are to be made. In Naafi, on the other hand, .the only common factor between one year and the next is that each proves to be surprisingly capricious and unpredictable as any other period in Naafi's history.'

By the late 50s, the town of Krefeld – northwest of Düsseldorf – became the epicentre of the food supply chain. Over 500 people worked at the Naafi depot there in jobs ranging from administration, pre-packing and the bakery to manning the fresh produce store, cold store for meat and fish, warehousing, and security. The Naafi commercial transport fleet consisted of 450 vehicles, covering 16 million kilometres annually.

The 1968 catalogue offered something for everyone.

Goods from the UK arrived by road, mainly on contractors trucks via Dover and Felixstowe. Tea from the Naafi's UK factory was collected once German wines had been delivered and unloaded at their warehouse in Amesbury. A container service at Rotterdam in Holland ferried in products from global suppliers, whilst continental producers delivered their wares directly to Krefeld.

From Krefeld, deliveries went to shops and clubs in Germany, Belgium, and Holland, along with a regular dispatch to Naples and Sardinia. Over 40 tons of Danish milk was collected six-times a week by Naafi vehicles. For the clubs, 230 tons of beer was dispatched weekly. The onsite bakery had an average weekly output of 85,000 loaves of bread, 80,000 rolls, and 100,000 pies. Fresh food staples including lettuce and tomatoes were purchased in Holland, but occasionally, producers in Germany were sometimes used.

***

Not long after Krefeld was opened, a new modern logo to replace the regimental crest was unveiled. It was the first visual identity change since 1921. The original Naafi crest embodied the emblems of the three Services—the foul anchor, the crown and the wings—symbolizing their triple loyalties.

The motto: 'Servitor Servientium' although not the best of Latin, means 'Servant of Those Who Serve.' Naafi used to tell staff not to interpret 'servant' in any derogatory sense. 'To serve our fellow men is the fundamental purpose of the Good Life; and when those fellow men happen to be the sailors, soldiers and airmen of our beloved Patron, Her Majesty the Queen, what finer cause could any good citizen hope to serve?'[125]

In fact, records show Naafi had launched a search for a new 'distinctive symbol' in 1946 to serve as a 'camp sign, club sign or direction board.' A meeting was held between institute officials, well-known artists, and industrial designers to consider producing a logo, which the board hoped would eventually be as familiar as the YMCA triangle. The upshot was that the forces should be given the chance in creating the design, so a competition was launched which attracted over 4,000 entries. Ten were finally selected, and three shortlisted – but none ever used. *Naafi News* noted that the institute was: 'not bound to adopt the winning design for its new symbol. In fact, it is generally agreed that excellent though the three

---

[125] Naafi and You. Staff working pamphlet, 1955.

designs are, none of them quite achieves the purpose if a permanent Naafi symbol.'

The three finalists from the Naafi logo competition, none were ever used.

Such was the success of the institute at this point, that foreign armies became keen students of its methods; with military missions touring Naafi's in the United Kingdom and abroad.

One establishment which created much excitement in Asia was on the site of a former rubber plantation in Malaya. In 1961, Naafi transformed the plantation into a 17,000 square feet shopping arcade – with a supermarket and restaurant - servicing the *28th Commonwealth Brigade* at Terendak Camp. The project took just nine months to build and was the biggest venture of its kind ever undertaken by the institute. It was also the first location in the Far East where Naafi had entered the world of women's fashion. The arcade boasted everything the

Serviceman's larder required, including frozen products from a 36ft refrigerator. The shops were situated under a canopy running all round a square, which provided shelter against the weather – there were also committee rooms for local organisations and a health clinic.

The in-house publication *Naafi Review* boasted that the central showroom was a shoppers 'Aladdin's Cave,' displaying:

> ...furniture, carpets, labour saving appliances, electrical goods, china and glassware, bicycles, motor scooters, sports equipment, outboard engines, gramophone records, cosmetics, camera an photographic equipment. The clothing shop stocks wide ranges of British and Continental styles in dresses, shoes, swim and beachwear. A special department handles children's clothing and footwear and there is also a complete men's outfitters with ready to wear suits, shirts, socks, underwear and leisurewear.[126]

'Not even Malacca town or some of the other big towns in Malaya can boast such an up-to-date shopping centre,' the *Malay Mail* reported. In addition to shopping, a British styled pub served snacks and refreshments on the 'gay verandas' just a minutes walk from the arcade.

The modernisation drive presented some enormous difficulties, especially given as the cost for freight and import duties in some countries was not absorbed by the customer.

Deciding what was deemed a reasonable price for the

---

[126] Naafi Review, Autumn 1961. Edition 32.

goods it sold often lead to complaints of overcharging.[127] However, there were some advantages, as unlike most supermarkets in Britain, its margins overseas were not being squeezed hard by ferocious competition and high rents.

Another more pressing concern lingering on the horizon came as *National Service* conscription gradually ended from 1960, with call-ups abolished in December that year, causing anxiety at Naafi about its own future - especially given the strength of the armed forces would fall from 700,000 to 375,000 - constituting a loss of 50 percent of customers by 1962.

As the last conscripts signed-on, Naafi shut 26 branches in Germany. At the same time, a committee was appointed to consider the administration of the institute. Headed by John Corbett, it found that Naafi was meeting an essential need of the armed forces and its basic concept a specialist purveyor should continue, but changes were needed to take account of the more sophisticated needs of servicemen—and their wives. 'It needs to become more sophisticated and diversified,' Secretary of State for War, John Profumo said, adding: 'There is a growing demand that Naafi should provide facilities to enable a greater diversity of trading to be undertaken.'

Naafi listened carefully, as a modern retailer it needed to reshape and ditch the lingering 'char and wad' image. Social centres were no longer to be referred to as 'canteens' instead, they were re-branded 'Junior Ranks Club' - units were authorised to erect 'signs incorporating a name of their choice such as the regimental title, nickname or battle honour.'

---

[127]After taking freight, warehousing, insurance, protective packaging, and extra refrigeration into account.

After 'many requests from servicemen' Naafi spruced up bar menus, an event picked up by the *Daily Mirror* which splashed the headline: 'Naafi to serve…WINE'. 'Many of the lads acquire a taste for wine through serving overseas,' a *War Office* spokesman told the newspaper, adding that managers would decide what kind of wine they would sell. Despite the huge effort to drive change, the choices available for eating and drinking in the new clubs varied depending on a range of factors, primarily the skill of those charged with food preparation. By the early sixties, steak and chips became the favoured dish of rank and file soldiers, replacing beans on toast, but bacon butties, chips and tea also remained top-sellers.

The biggest technological advance was the introduction of 'day and night coin-in-the-slot' vending machines. Dozens of pigeon-holes contained food on view behind glass doors openable when sixpence was inserted in a slot. Chicken pies, steak pies, sausage rolls, sandwiches and cakes, in addition to confectionary were always available. The first machine appeared at the Royal Navy base in Chatham in 1958, beginning a new trend in 24-hour catering. Eventually, Naafi mechanical vending machines dished out packets of bubble gum, sweets, hot and cold foods, cigarettes, film for cameras, milk and crisps, as well as splashing a half-cupful of lukewarm water into coffee powder mix. Condom automats became legal in 1983 and were gradually installed in the gent's toilets at most Naafi bars.

In kitchens, the 'infra-red ray' griller; a device capable of whipping-up a juicy steak in under two-minutes started to appear. For eggs, bacon, ham, hamburgers, tomatoes and similar dishes, there was a new electric griddle plate.

Despite improvements, one old problem continued to plague the canteens. Just like during the war, Naafi began asking staff to watch out for Servicemen who 'borrowed' knives, forks and spoons from their canteens as part of a drive to cut losses. In 1964 alone– Naafi had to replace more than 70,000 knives and forks and in Britain alone, the canteens lost 95,000 cups at a cost of £120,000.

> Losses and breakages have been mounting year by year. It is not malicious. Servicemen don't just pinch things for the sake of it; they simply borrow items from the Naafi when they need them.[128]

By the mid-sixties, five hundred Naafi outlets spread across the world from Christmas Island to the Jungles of Malaya were staffed by 24,000 men and women of twenty different nationalities.

From trendy cocktail bars to bowling alleys, Naafi offered it all; one observer noted it had 'bustled into the nuclear age, with its wine, West End dinners and it's affluent customers.'

Chairman, Humphrey Prideaux – the young officer noted for his gallant efforts in Dunkirk - declared in 1965 that Naafi aimed for 'fatter wallets' as servicemen enjoyed immense spending powers. He said the institute had become 'a self-contained giant', producing its own-brand goods, bottling 160 wines, running a car hire-purchase scheme and ten-pin bowling alleys. In December 1965, furs went on sale at Naafi shops in the United Kingdom for the first time, with the launch marked by a special *Fur Fortnight* at the Naafi in Tidworth, where the display showed a choice of jackets, capes, coats, and stoles, in musquash, Canadian squirrel, mink and Siberian squirrel. There were also hats made from lamb, fox and China

---

[128] Naafi spokesman in 'Naafi News,' January, 1965.

mink and fur collars for winter cloth coats - all in the latest styling and shades.

Prideaux noted that although sales had increased, the corporation faced pressure because of rising costs. However, investment in new projects like the construction of a £37,000 shopping centre at RAF Marham, aimed to 'keep up with civilian facilities' continued. Plans were mapped out for introducing family launderettes, along with home-helps, dry-cleaning, beauty and hairdressing salons, furniture removals, and increased credit facilities.

A few years earlier, Naafi had ruffled the feathers of petrol station owners in Marham after making incursions into the fuel business. When the institute opened a filling station there, the *Garage and Motor Agent*, the trade's independent newspaper, observed: 'Retailers are understandably concerned. Although it can be said that the RAF's Naafi venture smells unpleasantly of the State competing with commerce, it is doubtful whether many Naafi stations will appear.' Naafi said the petrol station was open only to Service people and was installed at the request of the RAF as the nearest private petrol station was some miles away. We will open up others if we are asked to but these will not compete with private enterprise,' a Naafi spokesman said.

Prideaux also kept a close eye on the weak domestic economy which had forced Defence Minister Denis Healey to reduce military spending in Germany and press the West German government for more financial support, as Bonn was obliged to contribute to the cost of maintaining the British Army of the Rhine. 'With Soviet planes soaring over Berlin, and Soviet tanks chewing up the Berlin highway, the West Germans are realising more than ever the BAOR's essential role,' the *Daily Mirror* remarked.

The foreign-exchange costs of the British army in Germany were slashed by £20million in 1966 by reducing ammunition stocks and cutting the civilian payroll by 10 percent.

Politicians like James Davidson demanded the total repatriation of troops and investment in housing and the *National Health Service*.[129] Michael Foot, a future leader of the Labour Party, hoped the Army in Germany would not expand at a time when the Americans were considering reductions.

For his part, Healey confirmed troops would stay after an uneasy compromise was reached with Bonn, but the situation was still critical. Naafi launched a 'Buy British' promotion in the summer of 1966 aimed at reducing the Deutschemark currency drain. Special 'British Weeks' at RAF Gutersloh and Wildenwrath attracted over 300,000 visitors and pleas to 'Buy British' were made on the airwaves of BFBS radio at the peak listening hour before *Two-Way Family Favourites*. The downside of the campaign was spelled out by Dennis Martin, the *Daily Mirror* correspondent in Bonn:

> But if the Servicemen are patriotic and take the plea to heart they will have to pay more for their beer, for German beer is cheaper than imported British beer. German and Japanese radios and cameras are cheaper, too.

American forces in Germany had experienced a similar situation back in 1960 when President Eisenhower ordered a 'Buy American' campaign, which hit hard at the

---

[129] Member for Aberdeenshire West.

PX, where shelves had been stocked with 30 percent of foreign-made goods. Some GIs and their families complained that German household goods, English biscuits and Danish beer were removed from stores. But, as one report noted: 'most accepted the philosophy and many German shopkeepers are jubilant. They hope the lack of foreign goods in the PX will bring Americans into their shops.'

It is worth noting that American servicemen had enjoyed an extremely favourable exchange rate in the sixties, but in the summer of 1971, President Nixon took the dollar off the gold standard, prompting a huge drop in the rate with the Deutsche Mark. Budget cuts and the cost of the Vietnam War had made life for US troops in Germany increasingly difficult. The exchange fluctuations meant that those who had shopped in the local German stores (known as spending 'on the economy') were forced back into the PX and commissary for groceries. Leisure activities and travel off-base became an expensive business and in areas like Berlin, GIs could often be seen using the Naafi, as way of a change. The arrangement worked both ways, as the American PX was a favourite destination for the British, where, Levis jeans, bourbon and some electrical goods were markedly cheaper.

Even in the face of a fragile national economy, the sixties were a golden time for Naafi in Germany which recorded bumper revenues.

Meanwhile, Naafi headquarters in Kennington had been a peculiar space ever since the end of the *Second World War*, as it continued to be detached from the forces. Paul Eggelton worked as accounts clerk on the 'Cyprus desk' there in the early sixties, where once a week the accounting information arrived from Nicosia and he would enter the data into ledgers. 'Mine was the expenses,' he recalled. 'It was the most boring time of my life, as I was very good at numbers, so the whole job would take me a day and for the other four days I did nothing.'[130]

Despite the seemingly dull work, rules were tight: 'I was not allowed to read or look at anybody's work. There were about 200 clerks for all the territories plus a head and assistant accountant and you could see so many clerks stretching the work to fit the time,' Eggelton recalled.

Staff did have the use of a well-stocked cafeteria on site and staff received voucher for lunch. 'There were also two tea breaks, which we loved, as they broke into the monotony. Once a month a book of stamps, collected from the Naafi post office, would come round the office for us to purchase stamps, they were real bargains.'

The days of ledgers were already numbered, as technological advances also changed the retail landscape; Naafi embraced computers like the *Honeywell* mainframe, using them for stock-taking and inventories. Naafi moved from paper-tape and valves through punched cards to the latest microchip technology and high-speed magnetic disc processing. As technology improved, these systems connected Naafi offices to cold stores, bonded warehouses, shops, transport depots and bakeries.

By the late 1980s, a new vast state-of-the–art distribution centre had been constructed at Kempen, north of Dusseldorf, which was seamlessly operated by computers.

The huge government shake-off of old Colonial defence commitments continued into the early seventies with the closure of military installations in South East Asia, the

---

[130] Interview with author Nathan Morley, 2017

Persian Gulf, and the Maldives.

Aden, a British Crown colony from 1937, had gained independence in 1963. It was there that Brinley 'Phil' Gibbon spent many happy days at the Naafi by *Steamer Point Lido*, which had a beach with shark nets; and evenings were lively at the *Sixty Nine Club* 'where everybody banged the rattan chairs at least three times before sitting down - to dislodge the bed bugs! – and made mini pyramids from the empty cans of Tiger beer.'[131]

The RAF had operated a huge aerodrome at Khormaksar with its *Hawker Hunters* and *Wessex* helicopters, and a nearby base included a medical centre, cinema, Naafi, offices, and shops as well as married quarters.

The pullout from Singapore in 1971 spelled the death knell for Naafi's beloved *Shackle Club* at Raffles Place, where, it was claimed the longest bar in the world once stood.[132] In Malaysia –the famed *Galloway Club* Kuala Lumpur was also shuttered, with the premises being handed over to the local *Armed Forces Trading Corporation*.

---

[131] Brinley 'Phil' Gibbon – 'Memories of RAF Khormaksar'
[132] The Shackle Club, which had for long boasted of having the longest bar in the world, stretching straight for 90 feet. *Coventry Evening Telegraph*, 8th November 1945

The Shackle Club, just after *World War Two*.

Naafi reckoned the new decade required a fresh dynamic image. For starters, at an event at the *Tower of London*, a sealed urn containing a frizzled wad of *Nelson Cake* and a pot of stewed tea was ceremoniously buried in the grounds. 'No matter what we do, the old char and wad image persists,' a Naafi executive joked to the journalists gathered to watch the spectacle. 'We hope that with this ceremony we can bury the old idea forever.'[133]

A few days later, Naafi continued to bury the past by claiming the tide was running against clubs being a place to just enjoy a beer or strike up a conversation. The modern servicemen, they said, preferred to spend their free time watching 'scantily-clad dollies' dancing to mind-blowing music.

To this end, workmen were instructed to lay-down black-and-white tiled chequered floors at some Naafi

---

[133] Naafi preserved some of its history in a special display of 400 exhibits in a permanent tribute at a small museum at Imperial Court. Items on show included an old delivery bike and wheelbarrow. The display was closed sometime in the mid-1980s.

clubs to be used as 'dance areas', along with small DJ boxes and silver glitter-balls. Agencies began providing go-go girls, pop groups, disc-jockey's and psychedelic lighting effects, with guardsmen in Chelsea being the first to experience it. 'It is not quite the sort of entertainment that the boys' dads remember from the old days,' a Naafi spokesman said.

Eyebrows were raised in other parts of the country as 'artistic strippers' began appearing at bases, as Naafi fought to win back customers that were seeking thrills off camp. When a strip show was held at *Bassingbourne Barracks* in Hertfordshire, takings jumped from the normal £90 to about £220. 'It is our job to give the serviceman what he wants,' said Reggie Meyers, the Regional Manager. 'I've been with the Naafi for 45 years, and I must say I've seen nothing like it...during the show, the bar shutters were pulled down so that female staff would not be forced to see anything that offended them. We've had no complaints from them either,' he added.

Scantily clad go-go girls had yet to arrive in Germany; where many female employees were being replaced by similar 'automated restaurants' to those introduced at Chatham two decades earlier.

The *Daily Mirror* lamented that 'instead of a smile and a clatter of cups, soldiers are served by whirring slot-machines.' One young corporal who walked into the new automat at Iserlohn barracks for the first time remarked that it 'looked like an amusement arcade.' 'The grub's OK,' he admitted, 'but that was always only half the reason for coming into the Naafi. You can't chat up a machine when you are feeling a bit lonely.'[134]

Away from the canteen, there was brisk business at the

---

[134] *Daily Mirror*, March 8th, 1971

Naafi financial services and insurance division,[135] where servicemen could secure household insurance, loans, higher purchase, motor cover, kit, and house contents insurance and car sales from special desks at 53 stores in the UK, Germany, Northern Ireland and Cyprus and through a telephone service centre.

Other schemes included discounts and rewards, such as stamp books – similar to *Green Shield*, made popular at Tesco.[136] Stamp rewards (usually kitchenware, food or discounts luxury goods) were published in the monthly *Naafi News* magazine, which, along with the *Sixth Sense* newspaper, became part of the fabric of life in Germany.

Like in the days of Cologne after the *First World War*, Naafi employees, along with British troops and their families were leading a life largely independent of the local community, be it at postings in Europe, Asia or the Middle East.

By the time the official 'occupation' ended and the German Federal Republic attained sovereignty in 1955, most British families had left the requisitioned accommodation, taken amid such controversy in 1945, and moved onto camps, which had become heavily-organised closed military societies. At these 'temporary homes,' the family and residential environments mirrored housing estates in the UK, with rows of two-bedroomed houses, front and back gardens, and a driveway.

Unmarried Naafi workers were usually billeted in dormitories on camp, but renting an apartment in the

---

[135] Naafi Insurance services had become a considerable operation by the mid-seventies and the entire department re-located to Nottingham in 1978.
[136] Naafi stamps could be cashed anywhere in the world. At the checkout customers were asked if they wanted stamps or discount. The discount was originally set at 5 percent, but was reduced to 3 percent in the 1980s before being abolished altogether.

local town was also common. For the servicemen, the everyday routine of regulated military life was surrounded by these small, self-sufficient communities. The bigger garrisons operated petrol stations, libraries, post offices, churches, laundrettes, hospitals, schools, sports facilities and even local BFBS radio stations.

And, despite the thawing in relations between the Allies and the German population, there were only ever scattered hints of British- German contacts – especially as life 'behind the wire' became the norm. For most locals, except those employed by the British, a look over the fence was the closest they would come to seeing life on the camps.

The occasional Open Day, air-show or military Tattoo did provide locals a heavily supervised closer peek at their foreign neighbours. Likewise, the British were active participants in the local winter carnivals, Christmas markets and the ever popular Oktoberfest, where collecting a stone beer-mug became a must-have souvenir of a posting. Bases also were active contributors to local charities.

But not everything was rosy. This conflict-free existence was occasionally interrupted by complaints about noise pollution, or the environmental damage made by manoeuvres, which saw huge tanks ploughing through the local countryside – and, from time to time, environmentalists staged protests outside garrisons.

A problem which always attracted the local media was the occasional alcohol-fuelled brawl, usually involving 'squaddies' at local pubs and taverns. Military Police could be seen out in force on Friday and Saturday evenings in most garrison towns. Many German publicans were given the direct telephone number to the police guardhouse, should tempers flare (most Naafi bar-staff knew the number off by heart).

***

In 1972, Naafi unveiled its showpiece supermarket at JHQ which boasted a whopping 14,000 square feet of floor space stuffed with £250,000 worth of stock, including over 300 unique Naafi brand lines like sausages, meat pies, butter, baked beans, and bakery goods. The store was adorned with yellow and green Day-Glo posters, brand new metallic checkouts - installed with dividend stamp dispensers – and operated by cashiers in their new off-brown chequered uniforms.

Lady Wheeler, the wife of Air Chief Marshall Sir Neil Wheeler, had the honour of opening the shop. The event was deemed of such importance that Naafi commissioned a sponsored 32-page 'super-store supplement' feature in the base's newspaper *Union Jack*. Attending the opening of 'the biggest Naafi in the world' was the last major duty carried out by Sir Humphrey Prideaux who gave up the chairmanship and retired from the board the following year.

The *Union Jack* feature provides some interesting tidbits about the JHQ project, which estimated takings to be £3million annually. For example, the white goods section was selling on average 30 washing machines, 10 deep freeze units, and 16 Hoovers every week. From his raised glass-enclosed office, food hall manager Andrew Richardson could maintain 'watchful control,' whilst sports department manager Frank Carrol was busy selling golfing accessories, which became his top earner.

The Naafi superstore JHQ in 1977 (Authors private collection)

Janet Heath, a representative of *Max Factor*, was appointed permanent beauty consultant, whilst Heinz Thompson acted as resident 'audio expert' in the 'hi-fi' sound studio.

The store was the obvious choice for a demonstration of Naafi competence to Margaret Thatcher when she dropped in for a visit when she was escorted from aisle to aisle, inspecting everything from LP records and shoes to neatly stacked boxes of washing powder. There were other innovations too, like the '*Convex* anti-theft mirrors,' installed at supermarkets in Germany, Malta, Gibraltar and Cyprus and Check-Out operators were using the latest *Sweda* mechanical cash registers.

To help shoppers deal with spiralling inflation, Naafi designated 1973 as 'Help the Housewife Year,' by keeping down the cost of basic items like eggs, fats, tea, and sugar. Naafi said: 'it could go on forever...if you help support your own organization'.

It was at JHQ where Naafi first entered the deep-freezer market by selling the upright models, whilst increasing their frozen food range. Although bulk shopping had yet become part of the psyche of the British housewife, the boom in freezers for private homes took just two years from 1969 -1971 to rocket from virtually nothing to big business.

Despite power cuts being the biggest fear of those reluctant to buy a freezer, British retailers like *Bejams*, rightly predicted frozen foods had all the hallmarks for massive growth.

Meanwhile, the Naafi's own tea factory in Amesbury, overseen by blender and buyer Bill Payne, continued turning out its unique blends of tea and coffee (and supplying tea to the Navy), whilst Naafi wine buyer, Major Dick Pinker, made sure half a dozen of its best selling wines were made available under their own symbol on supermarket shelves.

***

A few months before the Thatcher visit, Naafi had witnessed the ugliest internal dispute in its history when employee Bill Ingram claimed he was fired by the institute after submitting a report about 'illegal' Army trading at a camp in Germany.

Naafi members of the *Association of Scientific, Technical and Managerial Staffs* union (ASTMS) - mostly shop and club managers – turned out in freezing conditions to support Ingram, picketing outside the main entrance of the Krefeld distribution centre, causing widespread disruption. As 85 percent of the goods Naafi sold passed through Krefeld - supplying 163,000 customers –

including 40,000 families, the action had an immediate impact.

Three weeks into the strike, and increasingly frustrated by the impasse, anger increased when it was alleged German police attempted to break the picket line. On February 14th, police jostled with pickets and refused to allow them to persuade the drivers of trucks and other vehicles not to cross the line to the Naafi building

ASTMS sent an official protest to the Foreign Office and asked the union's vice-chairman, Doug Hoyle MP to raise the matter in parliament. Terry Comerford, the ASTMS official responsible for Naafi membership said it was, 'outrageous that German police should interfere in this way with British trade unionists striking against a British employer.'

But, three days after the scuffles, the situation took a dramatic turn for the worse when Naafi driver Sidney Carter drove his 30-ton fully loaded lorry over the picket-line, knocking down Peter Leadley, the manager of the Naafi at Dortmund, who was taking part in the strike.

Carter, a former Lieutenant-Colonel, faced two charges of causing bodily harm by wilful neglect. Leadley was transferred to a British hospital paralyzed from the waist down as a result of the injuries received.

Under mounting pressure, the strike ended on February 23rd, when Naafi and ASTMS agreed to settlement terms. In a BFBS radio broadcast, James Tannock, the manager of Naafi in Europe, pledged there would be 'no victimization' of any employee that took part in the strike, ASTMS would be given collective bargaining rights for its Naafi members, Bill Ingram was reinstated and strikers would be paid for the period of the dispute.

In July, Brigadier Eric Bailey, president of the court which consisted of three other officers and one civilian, acquitted Carter of causing bodily harm by wilful neglect. The verdict ended a five-day trial at Carnarvon Barracks which from heard more than 20 witnesses.

***

There was more drama the following year, when on August 24th, 1978, two bombs consisting of 130 kilos of high explosives were discovered in an abandoned car in the parking lot at JHQ.

Luckily, German and British experts were able to defuse the devices but had they exploded during shopping hours, serious injury and extensive material damage would have resulted. The explosive was the handiwork of the *Irish Republican Army* (IRA) as part of their armed paramilitary campaign against the British forces.[137] In response to the incident, a huge security clampdown was enacted with Service chiefs ordering that wives who used Naafi shops must produce their identity cards and offer shopping bags for inspection.

In fact, Naafi was no stranger to IRA campaigns. In March 1974, four bombs devastated Claro Barracks in Ripon, North Yorkshire, destroying the Naafi and leaving its manageress injured. Then, just a few months later, a massive 50-pound bomb was planted in the yard at *Imperial Court*. The device was discovered following a telephone tip-off only hours after Heathrow Airport was blasted by an even bigger bomb.

---

[137] A series of bombing attacks had occurred on or around British army installations in Germany during the evening of 18-19 August, 1978, causing extensive damage to property. Nine years later in 1987, thirty-one people were injured after a car bomb exploded outside the Officer's Mess in Rheindahlen (close to where the Naafi car park bomb was planted). The IRA later said it had carried out the bombing.

It wasn't just bombs that kept Naafi in the public eye. Few stories gripped the forces community as much as the mystery of missing British toddler Katrice Lee, who vanished without a trace from a Naafi supermarket on her second birthday on November 28th, 1981.

The incident happened at the Naafi in Schloss Neuhaus on the outskirts of Paderborn. The shop was not inside the military garrison, and without security.

Like most nightmares, it began innocently enough. The store was busy, as Katrice's mother shopped for party food on that fateful day. 'It (the Naafi) was packed with people as it was the last Army payday before Christmas. Katrice didn't want to sit in the trolley – she demanded to be carried, and I held her while we did the shopping,' her mother Sharon later recalled.

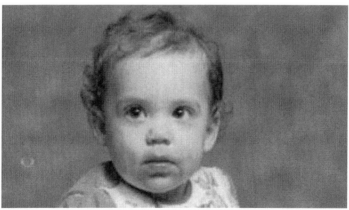

Katrice Lee

'We had started putting our shopping on to the conveyor belt. As I was getting the items out I realised I had forgotten to get crisps for the party. I put Katrice down and said to my sister, 'Just watch her while I nip back and get them.'

What happened next will probably never be fully established, as when she returned to the checkout, Katrice had vanished. 'The rest of the day was a blur. A military policewoman was at one of the other checkouts and radioed for assistance. Soon a full-scale search was underway.'

On the surface, it looked like action was immediate. A search took place in the area outside Naafi soon after her disappearance but came up empty-handed.

Given the severity of such a case, one would expect a rapid investigation. But what followed would come to haunt British Military Police, as a number of glaring oversights and incompetence emerged.

For one, it transpired that some Naafi checkout staff were not interviewed until six-weeks after the incident, incredibly, it later emerged that some never gave a statement at all. Border checks to neighbouring countries were not tightened directly after her disappearance either.

Theories abounded as to the fate of the missing toddler. Some concluded she was intentionally snatched and has possibly been raised by another family in Germany, Britain, or somewhere in Europe, and is unaware of her true identity.

As weeks became years and eventually decades, the family refused to give up hope.

In 2017, the Royal Military Police revealed an eyewitness saw a man carrying a small child in the area Katrice was taken from before putting her into a green saloon vehicle. At the same time, the Ministry of Defence reopened the case, finally admitting that its original investigation was flawed.[138]

---

[138] As of 2017, a re-investigation of the case, called Operation Bute was being carried out by Royal Military Police. At the same time, Sharon Lee

***

Those working in the front-line of Naafi operations could from time-to-time receive unexpected postings. That's what happened on January 5th, 1980, when three Naafi men were inoculated, vaccinated and became regular members of the RAOC. Then, they were then sent to RAF Brize Norton to catch a transporter destined for Salisbury in Rhodesia – and the beginning of *Operation Agila.*

A few months earlier, the *Lancaster House* talks had set Rhodesia on the path to democratic elections, but before the vote, an *International Ceasefire Monitoring Force,* was sent to man potentially dangerous assembly places where the forces of leadership rivals Robert Mugabe and Joshua Nkorno were gathering in vast numbers.

Captain John Perry, whose father is mentioned earlier in this book, along with Sergeant Phillip Lee and Corporal Allan Everest, were tasked to work with the Commonwealth troops in the peacekeeping force.

Their job was to establish and operate a Naafi-style supply unit, ferrying essentials to the 1,600 strong force in the capital and to remote areas in the countryside. Over 800 British soldiers, some 300 Royal Air Force personnel and a small number of Royal Navy and Royal Marines made up the peacekeepers, assisted by 150 Australians, 22 Fijians, 50 Kenyans, and 75 New Zealanders.

As in other countries, supplies ranged from confectionery to cleaning, and toilet goods. Delivery to some units presented particular problems. Many of the minor roads outside Salisbury were heavily mined, a

and her family were still campaigning for the release of the original police files.

danger Captain Perry witnessed first-hand. In one incident, he was not far behind the convoy in which Robert Mugabe was travelling when one of the cars exploded after driving over a mine.

Part of the risk came from the realities of deployment in a desperately unstable country. 'We were allocated arms in Britain and it was then that I think we began to fully grasp the situation,' Perry told *Naafi News* at the time. He said that in Salisbury - now known as Harare – 'it was not uncommon to see civilians walking around town with shotguns or carrying grenades in their belts, and there were men in the streets with obvious war injuries.'

Before the operation wound up in March 1980, a total of 46,0001bs of goods were flown out from the UK to Salisbury and distributed by Perry, Everest, and Lee.

CHAPTER 22
THE 80S AND FALKLANDS

THE BEGINNING of the eighties saw the new Thatcher government eye extensive cuts to the armed forces - and again just like in 1960 - Naafi feared the worst.

When Defence Secretary John Nott published his Defence Review, the military community was left stunned at proposals to whittle down the army in Germany to 55,000 and lay-off some 2,500 RAF airmen. The Royal Navy was to ditch aircraft carriers, lose one-fifth of its frigates and destroyers, and either privatise or close a number of naval dockyards.

At Naafi, rumours of privatisation or even closure became rife, especially given that deregulation was the watchword of the Thatcher administration.

However, in a 2017 interview, John Nott couldn't recall any changes to Naafi being discussed. 'I have no memory of dealing with this subject when I was a minister in the 1980s,' he said. 'And my junior Ministers for the armed forces have all passed away. I do not remember the issue of privatisation arising during my Defence Review and if it was considered I would have left it to the Army for decision.' [139]

But it was Nott's proposal to retire the ice patrol ship *Endurance* from the South Atlantic which caused genuine alarm – as it turned out to be an idea that would change history.

---

[139] Interview with Nathan Morley, 2017

Argentina's hawkish military junta followed the Defence Review with interest, as the country had for decades, claimed sovereignty over the relative backwater islands known as the Falklands, which was patrolled by the *Endurance*.

The Falkland Islands were - and remain - British overseas territory. Its landscape of windswept rocks and bogs juts 350 miles off the coast of Argentina, and has a total population of just over 1,800, of whom half lived in Port Stanley, the only town.

Misreading the *Endurance* decommissioning as a sign that Britain was ready to abandon the islands, Argentinean troops rolled onto the Falklands on Friday, April 2nd, 1982.

News of the occupation sent London into crisis. The Foreign Secretary quit. John Nott offered his resignation - but was told to remain in his post. Many politicians had reason to regret the constant talk of defence cuts. A vast naval task force of more than 100 ships was hastily cobbled together. The Naafi had only four days to ensure provisions for the messes and canteens, along with other supplies, were procured and loaded.

Dockyards across the south became hives of frenetic activity. Cranes swung crates onto the decks of *HMS Hermes, HMS Invincible* and countless other ships.

Massive volumes of cargo, including half a million eggs, over spilled warehouses. Delivery required a constant stream of trucks delivering day and night.

'We were working behind the scenes making sure the ships had everything they could possibly need,' recalled warehouse assistant Anne Holden, who was based in Plymouth.

Eventually the Naafi secured supplies for 25,000 men, as

well as the 8,000 soldiers and Marines bound for the islands.

The events of that time will remain forever etched into the memory of Kevin O'Kane, then a Canteen Manager on *HMS Broadsword*, en route to a deployment in the Persian Gulf: 'We were, of course, aware of the situation in the South Atlantic with Argentinean forces occupying South Georgia and the threat of worse to come,' he recalled, 'but as we were thousands of miles away and heading in the opposite direction, we never gave it much thought.'

O'Kane's plans for a summer in the tropics were short lived. The *Broadsword's* Captain announced the ship had been ordered to return to Gibraltar: 'In three hectic days we had rearmed, restored, changed warm weather kit for that more fitting for the cold South Atlantic and were prepared for war.'

Seawolf missiles tied to upper deck handrails alongside boxes of 40mm *Bofors* ammunition made an unforgettable sight.

'Health and safety rules were long forgotten as ammunition and equipment was stored wherever there was space,' O'Kane recalled.

On arrival at Ascension Island, beside the commotion and frantic activity of embarking yet more stores and weaponry, there was an incident of note regarding O'Kane and his canteen assistant.

> We were both called to the First Lieutenant's cabin and without preamble, given the choice of disembarking and flying back to the UK or signing on in the Royal Navy as 'Hostilities Only' ratings.

HMS Broadsword

Without hesitation, we both agreed and signed on the dotted line. In truth, we were the only real volunteers on that ship, having turned down the option denied to the enlisted men of going home should they so desire.

Kevin found the atmosphere on board hard to describe as the crew settled into a routine of permanent action stations.

We lived on pot mess, (stew), sandwiches and food that could - at a push - be eaten standing up. The cooks and caterers were outstanding. Despite bombs, bullets and anything else the Argies threw at us, there was always hot food and drinks available though it would be several weeks before we saw chips on the menu due to the risk of hot fat flying everywhere in the event of a hit on the galley and salads were a mere dream.

During lulls in the daytime action, my lad and I would fill a couple of boxes with drinks, chocolate, biscuits, snacks and the like from the canteen and go round to the various departments, saying to anyone who took something, 'Pay me later when it's over mate' and needless to say, most if not all, did though we did eventually run out of stock until a swiftly arranged replenishment at sea.

On May 25th, Argentine aircraft honed in on the *HMS Coventry*. Memories are still crystal clear for Kevin, who witnessed the attack from the deck of the *Broadsword:*

Earlier, *Coventry* had shot down three aircraft...our two ships came under sustained attack by four Skyhawk's in two separate passes, the first inflicting shell damage to both ships. *Broadsword* was struck by a 500lb bomb which bounced off the sea, passed through the side of the ship, and exited through the flight deck, [taking the nose off a helicopter] before vanishing over the other side and exploding harmlessly in the sea. At this point, we had no idea what had happened.

It was a terrifying experience...none of us had heard a bomb explode before. ...Hearing this enormous banging, crashing sound, we assumed it had gone off and that we were, quite literally, sunk!

It wasn't until some minutes later that a member of the damage control team, no doubt under strict orders, ventured through the watertight door. [He] took one look at the huge gash in the ship's side, and the hole in the flight deck, with water flooding in from a burst fire main, and reported that a bomb had hit the ship but hadn't exploded.

We were still fighting the ship at this time and couldn't really do anything about the damage, so some twenty-five personnel, [including] myself had no choice but to lie there, thirty feet away from what we thought was an unexploded bomb. It was only after the second raid passed that it was determined that the bomb had passed right through the ship without exploding.

What happened next happened quickly.

The second and more determined attack was devastating. With four aircraft attacking in two waves, *Coventry*, in an attempt to bring her Sea Dart missiles to bear or as a result of a communications error, pulled in front of *Broadsword*, effectively blocking the arc of fire from our for'ard Seawolf missiles which had locked on to the attacking aircraft.

Catastrophe resulted. Three bombs tore through the *Coventry*. The ship overturned and sank within twenty minutes. Nineteen lives sank with it. It fell to *Broadsword* to rescue the *Coventry's* surviving crew. Again, Kevin O'Kane provides account:

I was dispatched, first as part of the triage team, filtering the seriously wounded and those less so to the relevant first aid stations. It was hugely inspiring to see those less affected look after their own shipmates who were obviously deep in shock, burying themselves in blankets shaking and blank-eyed with the horror of what had just befallen them. We worked frantically to comfort them, get them warm and dried and eventually fed and rested... And, it has to be said, giving the odd 'tot' or two where it was needed.

I found my counterpart, the Canteen Manager of *Coventry*, huddled in one of the messes. His name was Ron. He was in the same state as the others: cold, wet and shocked – but glad to be alive. I took care of him, got him showered and into dry clothes... [I got him] fed and watered. I fixed him up with the essentials like soap, toothpaste and the like from the canteen—which was wide open for everyone to do the same—and eventually saw him off with the others to the Hospital ship Uganda. As they were transferred by landing craft and [helicopter] there was a loud shout of 'Three Cheers for the *Broadsword*' and over 150 voices cheered us as they departed.

Following the 25th May attack, our fighting days were effectively over. We were dispatched north to repair our damage. As our weapons systems, apart from the helicopter, were still operative, we were again allocated the role as 'goalkeeper' to

HMS Hermes. [We] survived the rest of that conflict without seeing further action.

Even after the white flag [flew] over Port Stanley and the land forces surrendered, we couldn't stand down. We were uncertain if the military junta in Argentina were ready to give up the fight, [if they'd] instructed their air force to stand down. Eventually, it was over. [All] the other ships in the area…witnessed a victory fly-past of the remaining Harriers and helicopters over Port Stanley. After many weeks the Chief's Mess bar— which though never officially closed, [was] rarely used—fully opened. To this day I remember the hangover which followed!

In the Falklands War, an EFI detachment served with the Task Force. John Leake, who had worked for Naafi since 1977, won the *Distinguished Service Medal* for his gallantry while manning an anti-aircraft machine gun on board *HMS Ardent*.

Major General Julian Thompson, commander of British Land Forces said: 'Naafi's swift response to the Falklands War was not unexpected to those of us who had been around long enough to know what their staff had achieved in various campaigns around the world. We took it for granted that Naafi wouldn't let us down. We were not disappointed. There is something very reassuring about seeing Naafi carrying on despite bombs, bad weather and enemy aircraft.'

With the end of hostilities, the main Naafi was set up out towards the old airport, which became RAF Stanley. It stood in an area called the 'Canache,' which also housed the Globe cinema, the *Victory Club* and the Naafi bar. Even now, Naafi in the Falklands continues to serve thousands of soldiers and airmen posted there on a four-month basis. A correspondent, visiting Ports Stanley in 1985, noted:

> There is a military presence, apart from the small rest and recreation camp on a hillside. Rapier ground to air missiles, one of the Godsends of 82, and 105 batteries guard the approaches, as they do throughout the Falklands - backed up by naval frigates, submarines, Phantoms, Harriers, Chinook helicopters and the rest of the *Fortress Falkland's* arsenal which has altered a lifestyle.

CHAPTER 23
THE 90S

ONE successful improvement for the lives of service families in Germany came in the form of the *Britannia Centre* which replaced the ageing *Summit House* as the main Naafi in Berlin in 1990.

The red-brick supermarket was built on the site of *Spandau Prison*, which had been torn down after the death of its lone inmate Rudolf Hess, Hitler's former deputy.

Wittily, customers christened the new centre *Hessco*. Captain Birdseye was flown in to 'personally hand out teddy bears' to 200 lucky customers on the opening day (provided their parents had purchased a Birdseye product).

But, the paint had hardly dried on the gleaming new complex, when, on the night of November 9th, 1989, the *Berlin Wall* - which separated East Germany from the West - came tumbling down.

Images of tens of thousands of delirious citizens pouring in both directions and dancing atop of the wall, defined this pivotal moment in world history. An Irish reporter in the city observed: 'In what was described as the biggest party that fun-loving Berliners had ever had, tens of thousands of East and West Berliners reunited in 11 raucous outpouring of joy that lasted all night.' None of the hundreds of British personnel who braved the cold that evening to celebrate with the locals, could have imagined the chain of events being triggered, as the *Warsaw Pact*, *Cold War*, and Soviet Union began to disintegrate. When the *Cold War* ended, there were still massive Allied military installations scattered across Germany.

The Americans had over 780 military bases and facilities in the Federal Republic and West Berlin, with over 550,000 soldiers, dependents and civilian employees.

A grand opening in Berlin, with Captain Birdseye.

Events in Eastern Europe provided the Thatcher government a 'peace dividend' and the opportunity to embark on huge military reductions. The late Alan Clark, then defence procurement minister, noted, 'We are at one of those critical moments in defence policy that occur only once every fifty years.'

That moment spawned a programme named *Options for Change* which proposed slashing military manpower by 18 percent, whilst retaining four *Trident* submarines, halving forces in Germany, with closures of facilities and bases in the Rhineland to continue through the nineties.

However, just as in 1982 during the Falklands crisis, conflict interrupted the new defence plan when a Middle Eastern despot ordered his army to invade and annex Kuwait on August 2nd, 1990. Over the next seven months, Iraqi leader Saddam Hussein—until that point never considered a threat to global security—ordered his troops to loot Kuwait's vast wealth, and plunder anything which could be transported. Iraq then installed a brutal occupation government. In response, then-US President George Bush bolstered his military presence in the Persian Gulf. In all, over 200,000 American troops were deployed, along with 150,000 from many Allied nations. For the British, this mission was known as *Operation Granby* and involved over 50,000 troops, the majority deployed from bases in Germany.

As the troops headed east, a canteen on wheels opened up at in the German port of Bremerhaven to serve the 7th Armoured Brigade. Just like on D-Day 46-years earlier, Naafi handed out ration packs to soldiers on the move.

As expected, Naafi, wearing the EFI badge, also deployed on the ground—70-volunteers in all, stepped forward from the UK and Germany, with the first team setting up shop, quite literally, in giant tents and truck containers on the Saudi – Kuwait border.

Kevin Royle, with EFI, remembers being briefed about the threat of chemical warfare:

> We were all issued with NBC suits and other necessary items and given lectures to ensure we understood the requirements. Likewise weapons and ammunition, with some range shooting practice. On the ground during the build-up to the war we were kept up to date with daily meetings so that everyone knew what was going on and when things would kick-off.

As troops strengthened their grip in the desert, Naafi dished out goods at two 24-hour shops and canteens. Royle recalls an atmosphere of concentrated effort.

> We originally deployed as seven in number but as the number of troops increased we were hard pressed to cope. This was partly due to no decent premises and no store. We initially operated from a small shop/office facility, until we became part of the logistic company compound. No 'warehousing' just an area of containers which grew as our shipments arrived from the UK. We set up facilities in tentage in the troop camp areas and ran mobile facilities to desert locations. Our numbers were increased as troops increased.

The public relations department at *Imperial Court* churned out data-stuffed reports about supplies and consumption, with one notable item; to wit, that soldiers spent over

£30,000 on sending flowers and chocolates to their loved ones via a special Naafi-*Interflora* service. Certainly, Naafi knew how to use a press-opportunity to its best advantage, with any story from the Kuwaiti theatre greedily lapped up by *Fleet Street*.

In January 1991, after months of failed diplomacy and troops battling boredom in the desert, the deafening sounds of Allied bombing suddenly shook Iraq - an all-out onslaught was beginning. The confrontation would be the first salvo of the Gulf War. Over the next 30 days, Iraq became used to devastation from the air. Then, in February, Allied forces launched a combined land, air, and sea assault. 'Overall it was a hard-pressed time for all of us,' Royle adds. 'With most working seven days a week until 10/11 pm, and then being woken by alarms about incoming Skud missiles, and then having to go to our bomb shelter, fully clothed in NBC kit. During the run-up to war, no one got changed to go to bed!'

It soon became clear that Iraq was suffering a terrible defeat and their troops scurried from Kuwait. By the middle of May, many British soldiers had packed up their tents and returned to home bases in the UK and Germany. Kevin Royle was one of them:

> Our time spent in the Gulf was 'dry,' no alcohol whatsoever, it was afterwards that we realised that we could not be alcoholics! On the aircraft home, we were given, with our packed meal, a small bottle of wine and a can of lager. The whole of the aircraft was half cut in about ten minutes!

Some men remained in theatre (including 11 EFI members) to participate in *Operation Safe Haven*, a mission to defend Kurds fleeing their homes in northern Iraq and deliver humanitarian aid to them. Of the 47 British soldiers who died during the conflict, nine were killed by so-called American 'friendly fire' when US planes mistakenly attacked two British armoured vehicles.

The Gulf conflict had a deep economic impact on the institute, with trade in Germany falling dramatically. Roger Lyons, assistant general secretary of the *Manufacturing, Science and Finance Union*, which represented 2,000 of 10,000 Naafi workers, warned that the future for the institute was bleak. He believed that the main problems affecting profits were the increased commercial activities of regimental clubs: 'This could be a terminal crisis,' he warned. Naafi rejected the claim, although a spokesman told the *Guardian* it was 'engaged in an ongoing review of our business strategy.'

In 1992, the Naafi left *Imperial Court* and by 1995, for the first time in its history, Naafi recorded losses to the tune of £1.9 million, with the haemorrhaging topping £4 million the following year.

As might be expected, the government took note, with Defence Secretary Michael Portillo drafting in Geoffrey Dart, a skilled retailer from Marks *and Spencer* to revitalise the business and pare back costs. Naafi's days as the all-conquering retailer to the forces were over, as pile-it-high-sell-it cheap supermarkets like Tesco and Sainsbury's mushroomed across the UK. 'We recognised that junior service people do have a lot of choice,' Naafi chairman David Roberts lamented at the time. 'The idea that Naafi has a monopoly is hogwash. Most personnel have cars or motorbikes or can pay for taxis. If we don't provide what they want, they will find someone else that will.'

The situation was similar in Germany, where huge

discount retailers sprung up in garrison towns including Gutersloh, Herford, and Bielefeld.

As was the case in the early 80s, the threat of closure loomed. If Naafi could not be saved, it would simply be ditched. With this in mind, Dart began orchestrating a restructuring focusing on the organisation's traditional core activities; namely, shops and clubs. He complained that forces shops looked ghastly with their poorly lit interiors and linoleum floors. 'They had bad ceilings, bad furniture, and poor refrigeration,' he observed. His conclusion was that outside alliances with high street stores and leading breweries needed to be formed to help turn the situation around.

Spar, one of the oldest names in retail, won the contract to operate convenience stores; they quickly re-branded 200 Naafi shops in the UK at a cost of £10 million. The arrangement was such that Naafi paid Spar for 'specialist retailing services,' including warehousing, distribution, point-of-sale equipment, and marketing.

Naafi, however, provided the staff and kept the profits. The formula worked and by 1998 sales had jumped by more than 40 percent. Spar also taught Naafi staff everything from bacon slicing to shop management. Spar had an impressive track record - by the late 60s they were operating 3,500 shops in Britain, most stocked with their own branded products. By the 90s, the chain was present in 20 countries on four continents.

Elsewhere, many of the antiquated clubs were converted to pubs after an alliance was formed with *Bass, McEwan's,* and *Newcastle Breweries.* Prior to the changes, Dart described the clubs as being 'very big, very dark, and very depressing.'

In all, 228 clubs were refurbished and re-branded. The brewers provided training, industry knowledge, and marketing, while Naafi supplied staff.

But it was not all good news. In 1994, Naafi gained a three-year contract to supply food to service units as part of a Ministry of Defence effort to amalgamate the food supply to troops. The contract, which it won without having to fight any rival bids, was a Godsend, especially as a drop in sales in Germany, due to the reduction in forces there, was beginning to pinch. The contract represented one-quarter of Naafi business.

Unfortunately, things quickly soured. Within months of the new arrangement, a computer glitch caused deliveries to units to be delayed, and in some cases missed altogether. A select committee described the situation as a 'minor debacle' and complained that troops were not receiving an acceptable standard of service. MPs said: 'Overall service continued to fall short of the performance standard required by the contract in a number of respects.' They also expressed 'dismay at the extent of difficulties encountered' and warned troops that they may have to sustain the brunt of any losses made by Naafi. On one occasion, a missed food delivery to a naval base resulted in the entire unit eating dinner at a local McDonald's.

Unsurprisingly, when it expired in 1997, the contract was awarded to a private company, *Booker Foodservices*. Naafi claimed that the lost contract cost them 2,000 jobs.

But, despite the setback, the institute continued to enjoy government support. Speaking in the House of Lords on in 1997, Earl Howe said:

> The future importance of Naafi to the services cannot be overstated. Naafi now has a chief executive who is determined to drive the organisation forward, to modernise and to make

sure that its services are consistent with what our Armed Forces wish to receive. I have every confidence in Naafi's ability to do that and every confidence that the restructuring exercise that I mentioned will enable it to invest to the degree necessary to ensure that the clubs in particular but also the retail outlets are upgraded to a satisfactory standard.

On a lighter note, a year earlier, the Naafi marked their 75th anniversary and was in receipt of a special message from Buckingham Palace.

I send my warmest regards to all the staff and pensioners who have so loyally served the Armed Forces. I first visited the Naafi in January 1946 when, as Princess Elizabeth, I opened the Naafi club at Portsmouth.

My father, King George VI, granted his Patronage in 1947 in recognition of the achievements of the Naafi during the *Second World War.* I was pleased to continue that Patronage upon my accession and my family and I have seen Naafi in action on our many visits to Service establishments throughout the world.

In today's world, the role of our Armed Forces is continually developing. As I watched the Naafi float during the VJ Day Tribute and Parade, I was reminded of the loyal service you provide, whatever the circumstances.

In your 75th anniversary year, I thank you for your message of loyal greetings and for the past years of dedicated service to the Armed Forces of the United Kingdom. I wish you every success in the future.

ELIZABETH R.
January 1996

CHAPTER 24
AFGHANISTAN & IRAQ

AFTER weathering their biggest challenge for a generation, Naafi re-branded in 2000 with a new patriotic red, white and blue logo. 'It is a bold statement we are making and a measure of the progress the company has made in three years,' beamed Simon Monkman, the Head of Brands and Communication. 'We now wear the Naafi badge with pride and we believe it will be regarded as a seal of quality and trust among the British Armed Forces.' Optimism was spurred after Naafi roared back to profitability, sales at UK stores up 13 percent - turning in a profit of nearly £2 million.

It seemed that despite accusations of being uncompetitive and outdated, the institute still had the agility to thrive, and a flurry of fresh ideas followed. First off was the construction of a 'Naafi Max' shopping village at Paderborn in Germany, with a plush food hall; a home and leisure department; travel agent; jeweller; 24-hour dry cleaner; hairdresser and café. The 'Naafi Max' formula was basically a shopping mall in miniature, with franchised food outlets and cafes - customers at Colchester were 'launched into cyberspace' where the first internet café opened. In the same period, Tesco branded products appeared on shelves at stores in Germany, Cyprus, and the Falkland Islands.

Spar continued to be instrumental, providing buying, marketing, logistics, information technology support services, as well as a range of products including Spar branded goods. In another major development, Naafi opened a state-of-the-art retail facility on-board aircraft carrier *HMS Invincible*, whilst at the same time appointing Beverley Parkinson as its first-ever female Naval Canteen Manager when she took charge of the canteen on-board *HMS Liverpool.*

The institute also signed a deal with the telecommunications company, *Servi-Tel* to provide 'Keeping in Touch' (KIT) cards, designed exclusively for Servicemen to keep in touch with family and friends when posted overseas. The KIT phone-cards could be bought in denominations of £5 and £10, and used from any touch-tone phone. Customers simply dialled an 0800 number which asked them to enter the pin-number on their card. Then, they heard a dialling tone and could phone the number they required.

Another strategic review concluded that Forces in the UK and overseas had 'very different' requirements. In Great Britain – competition was high because of the wider range of retail and leisure choices provided by the local community. With that in mind, Naafi was split into two divisions; Naafi International, serving 48 military overseas bases and Naafi GB, which would whittle down commitments on 151 military bases in the UK.[140]

The launching of this new structure came as Naafi staff - wearing EFI uniform - served in Bosnia, Croatia, Kosovo, Macedonia, Kuwait, Italy, Saudi Arabia, and Sierra Leone.

Naval Canteen Service staff on-board *HMS Invincible* in the Balkans were recognised with the NATO Medal for

---

[140] Naafi GB was to operate in England, Scotland and Wales, where its facilities were used significantly less because of the wider range of retail services available to the Forces in the UK. Northern Ireland, overseas military bases, the Expeditionary Force Institutes (EFI) and the Naval Canteen Service (NCS) was to be managed through Naafi International.

service in Kosovo. In Kosovo itself, the *Expeditionary Force Institutes* ran six clubs and three shops.

'I am very proud of our NCS staff. While it is, by no means, obligatory for them to remain on-board ship in times of war, it is a testament to their spirit that, in all recent hostilities, our canteen staff have stayed with their shipmates,' remarked Peter Bott, Naafi Head of Operations.

At the same time, the biggest deployment of British Troops since the Gulf War was mounted across Oman, with EFI sending 34 members to run eight shops and canteens serving 15,000 men. Staff serving in the shop at Sha'afa had a surprise when Tony Blair, the then British Prime Minister, popped in during a brief tour. 'He was very nice and a lot taller than he looks on television,' EFI Lance Corporal Tracy Gun said.

Afghanistan, however, was another matter altogether. In 2002, Naafi donned the khaki again when *Operation Veritas*, a mission providing support to the vicious and prolonged War in that country commenced, beginning an almost continuous British presence there spanning the Blair, Cameron, and May governments.

On a cold January day in 2002, Naafi Brize Norton's Gill French and Nicole Taylor waved off troops from 2nd Battalion, The Parachute Regiment, Gurkhas and the Royal Engineers with warm winter cheer, serving Naafi tea and cakes before their long journey to Kabul.

Sergeant Sarah Walker, Lance Corporals Steve Muirhead and Derek Carruthers who as part of Naafi's *Expeditionary Force Institutes* soon followed to operate a shop serving all the troops contributing to the international security force.

Even today, British troops remain part of the NATO force helping the country's government fight a resurgent Taliban.

The early days of *Operation Veritas* were reminiscent to scenes witnessed 87-years earlier near the trenches of France. 'When we first got into Afghanistan in 2001, we just had a *Land Rover* with a trailer and went into Kabul where the armoured vehicles and troops were, and sold stuff out of the back of the wagon,' recalled EFI Sergeant Michael Corker. [141] Naafi shops were spread between the forbidding deserts and mountain ranges in places like Gereshk, Lashkar Gah and in areas of Helmand province, such as Sangin and at the sprawling Camp Bastion, where at its peak; it served 40,000 people supporting 600 daily aircraft and helicopter movements.

'Its hard work when you've got rockets flying around, but you've got your body armour and protection. You get used to the rockets, but you never get used to the weight of the armour and the heat,' Corker added.

Artist David L. Scholes reminisced about his experiences with the territorial's in Afghanistan, portraying a turbulent and divided nation. 'I found just a tiny Naafi shop, which provided posters, magazines and other reading material, as well as sweets and soft drinks. This being the only entertainment available, it was always packed with soldiers buying up in anticipation of a sugar high, and pouring through the newspaper headlines in an attempt to connect with home. If Iraq had been another world, arriving in Afghanistan was like returning to the Dark Ages.' [142]

Naafi also helped transform *Ukheyl School* on the outskirts of Kabul into one of the most modern in Afghanistan, when along with the help of the Royal

---

[141] 'Selling Pot Noodles on Afghanistan's front line.' Defence Focus, August, 2010.
[142] Without Prejudice: Iraq, Afghanistan: A Personal Account of Nations in Conflict By David L. Scholes.

Logistics Corps; the institute supplied furnishings, books, and stationery to help get the school back on its feet. 'The EFI makes a real difference to members of the British Armed Forces and in Afghanistan, this is particularly true. We are proud to support this military initiative and the provision of decent education supplies for these youngsters is a legacy that will remain for many years to come,' Colonel Murray Smith, Commanding Officer, EFI said.

Even though the UK withdrew the last of its combat troops in October 2014, a small British deployment of about 500 personnel remains to provide security around the capital Kabul.

***

By early 2003, another war with Iraq looked inevitable. The UN's chief weapons inspector Hans Blix said Saddam Hussein's claims to be disarming were a sham – a charge that would come back to haunt Britain and the United States.

At the time, Blix said Iraq failed to answer questions about its chemical, biological and missile arms programmes and was blocking his inspectors' efforts to find out what was happening in the country.

After a damning report by Blix, London and Washington said that they held out no prospect of Iraq complying with demands to prove it had destroyed its arsenal of 'weapons of mass destruction'. Hussein was accused of hiding missiles, biological and chemical agents, including VX nerve gas and anthrax.

The invasion began on March 20th, 2003, when the US, along with the United Kingdom and several coalition allies, launched a so-called 'shock and awe' bombing campaign. Under-equipped and badly trained Iraqi forces were quickly overwhelmed as the Allies swept through the country, leading to the collapse of the government; and the eventual capture of Hussein, who was found hiding in a bunker.

The invasion of Iraq eventually became an unpopular occupation. Naafi staff donned desert combat uniforms - and issued SA80 rifles. Much of the food and drink was delivered at high risk to truck drivers who ran the gauntlet of hostile villagers lining the route to some of the more remote outposts.

'It has been difficult getting food to bases in places like Al Amarah as the security situation has got worse,' a Naafi spokeswoman said at the time. 'Sometimes the convoys have not been able to get through safely so the supplies have been sent by helicopter. 'More than 50 truck windscreens have been lost on convoys because of stones being thrown at them.'

EFI operated warehouses at the Basra Palace Hotel and the Shatt-al-Aran Hotel. Eventually, shops were running at Camp Fox, Camp Centurion, Camp Beuhring, and in Basrah and Umm Qsar. At the height of the occupation, there were 46,000 British troops in Iraq leading to bumper profits in 2003.

In fact, troops in Iraq wolfed down so many Pringles that the packets would stretch for more than 10 miles if laid end to end, other favourites included *Pepperami,* which sold 47,000 units and vast quantities of *Coca-Cola.* Operations ended in Iraq in early 2009, with Naafi shutting up their last branch at Camp Beuhring in August of that year.

Back in Europe, main Naafi shops had began to expand their product range to include DVD recorders, plasma screen TV's and mountain bikes. In 2004, sales grew in Germany by 2.5 percent and the bestsellers that year included 212,172 DVDs and 203,379 tins of Heinz Beans.

Soon after, the chip and pin payment method was enforced in all German Naafi outlets, whilst the institute also started to offer consumers a re-useable 'Bag for Life' in a number of stores.

Another popular addition to the shelves was its own label brand tea, featuring distinctive retro-style packaging displaying the historic Naafi crest.

Naafi tea makes a return.

The old 'char and wad' image that Naafi had tried to bury in the sixties, returned with a nostalgic bang. 'For us, the key is to provide British products which offer good, honest value and our products are based on a unique point of difference such as 'the biggest,' 'the best' and 'truly memorable,' CEO Reg Curtis said when the tea was officially launched.

CHAPTER 25
THE FUTURE

IN 2007, Naafi reduced its executive structure, whilst 'reassessing its strategic direction,' as the scale of the business fell in terms of turnover, operating locations, and headcount.

Today, the institute operates in far fewer locations but is still present in Germany, Gibraltar, Brunei, and the South Atlantic Islands and on board HM Ships.

With around 100 outlets, it still provides a 'taste of home' to Forces and their families overseas.

In 2013, sixty-years after opening, Naafi's main store in Germany closed their doors for good, as units slowly left Rheindahlen. The closure didn't herald a clearance sale - as the stock was moved to other branches, along with some of its workforce.

The final bargains were in the form of a few sweets and pasties, nearing their sell-by date.

The population at JHQ had fallen from 9,000 to a few hundred by 2013, and the upper floors and much of the old retail space had been sealed off as customer numbers dwindled. 'On a Friday afternoon, Saturday or Sunday, you couldn't park in the car park, that's how busy it was,' one customer told Forces television on its last day. 'People used to travel right across Germany to come to this Naafi, because it was the biggest and best in Germany. The Naafi has been an integral part and supported community,' another shopper lamented.

The branch, famously toured by Margaret Thatcher and the former Jewel in the Naafi crown, shut without fanfare

- the manager said there was nothing left to sell. Fixtures and fittings were loaded onto several trucks and sent into storage.

The headquarters for British Forces in Germany moved from Rheindahlen to Catterick Barracks Bielefeld, as Celle and Münster stations closed and the estates were handed back to German Federal authorities.

A year later in 2014, Hameln station was shut, with the disbandment of *28 Engineer Regiment.*

Closures of garrisons at Bergen-Hohne, Elmpt, Fallingbostel, and Herford followed. Small parts of Paderborn and Gütersloh remained operational, but much of the garrisons were handed back or closed.

As the decade rolled on, it became clear the withdrawal of the British was leaving a huge void in many communities. Some former bases became new residential areas for the locals or industrial estates, others turned into ghost towns. The station at JHQ was used to house hundreds of refugees escaping the conflict in Syria. Soon after, the bulldozer tore down the last reminders of its former occupants.

In December 2017, Naafi embarked on probably their last venture in Germany when they became partners in a small shop-cafe called 'The Buzzard' at Ayrshire Barracks near Monchengladbach - the last base slated to remain open before the complete draw-down. The shop, providing a 'taste of home', serves troops working on the 1,000 armoured and support vehicles kept in climate controlled warehouses, on standby for emergency deployments.

The last British Field Army units will return to Britain from Germany in 2019. Currently, there has been no decision on Naafi's future post 2020. But, as it stands 'Service Level Agreements' remain in place in all the territories where they currently operate until 30th April, 2020, with the exception of Northern Ireland, which was handed over to Carillion/Aramark in late 2017. The latter being part of the MOD/DIO 'Project Hestia' which is harmonising the provision of soft facilities management across the UK defence estate and ends 48-years of service to the forces and their families in The Province.

So, for now at least, it is reassuring to know that when British Forces need rest and refreshment at home, abroad or at sea, Naafi still remains at hand, upholding its motto, 'Servitor Servientium' - *The Servant of Those Who Serve.*

CHAPTER 26
SIXTH SENSE ARTICLE

The article below was published in the final ever edition of the British Forces newspaper *Sixth Sense* in Germany on December 14th, 2017.

Naafi holds unique place in the history of British Forces Germany

One thing I quickly discovered when embarking on a history of the Naafi is that nearly everyone has an opinion about it. To be sure, some are less favourable than others, although even Naafi's worst critics show it a grudging regard. For instance, few would dispute that it occupies a unique place in British history.

Moreover, charting its story has turned up many interesting untold tales. When Sixth Sense launched in 1970, Naafi was going through what we would now call "corporate re-branding." In the winter of that year, a sense of astonishment prevailed as eye-grabbing articles appeared about go-go girls, miniskirts, and late night parties at the Naafi.

Surprisingly, it was all above board. The institute was dragging itself into the seventies, insisting, "today's Servicemen prefer scantily-clad dollies dancing to mind-blowing music." To that end, agencies provided Naafi with go-go girls, pop groups, disc jockeys, and "psychedelic lighting" effects at their clubs in London.

In Germany around the same time developments were somewhat less thrilling, with the introduction of "automated restaurants." As one correspondent suggested then, "chatting up the birds serving tea and buns in the Naafi was in serious danger of becoming a lost military art." Now, instead of a smile and the clatter of cups, servicemen in Germany were served by "whirring slot-machines."

"It looks like an amusement arcade," a young soldier at a camp in Iserlohn bemoaned. "The grub's OK, but that was always only half the reason for coming into the Naafi. You can't chat up a machine when you are feeling a bit lonely."

There were other problems too. Many managers had to rely upon their ingenuity to distract customers from the drabness of the scruffier clubs. In the mid-seventies, a young airman serving Gutersloh remarked that the décor at his local Naafi bar left a lot to be desired. Yet, he added, it was warm and had a TV, which, "despite the programmes all being German, brightened up our evenings."

Even this was an improvement on the canteens that served a generation of national servicemen during the 50s and 60s. Actor Johnny Briggs (based at Paderborn) as well as musician Aker Bilk both admitted to using their local Naafi as a base to arrange the flogging of chocolate, coffee, and cigarettes to the local population.

Despite the best efforts of its public relations department, a constant stream of stories featuring Naafi kept it in the press—many papers even had full-time correspondents based in Germany.

By the end of the Second World War, Naafi had reached its zenith with canteens, shops, and clubs on all seven continents and over 120,000 employees on the payroll. It was also one of the largest trading organizations on earth. In Germany alone (undoubtedly the "jewel" in the Naafi crown), clubs, canteens, and shops operated in Hamburg, Berlin, Bielefeld, Celle, Dortmund, Düsseldorf, Gutersloh, Hanover, Herford, Krefeld, Munster, Osnabruck, Hameln, and Oldenburg.

After the war, the British Army of the Rhine mushroomed into a vast organisation, employing, in addition to military personnel, logistic, administrative, education, and welfare professionals.

The first military wives arrived in 1946. With this new huge customer base, Naafi tried to copy the changes seen in British consumer habits by overhauling their scruffy counter service branches with the aim of becoming a "glossy combination of supermarket and club."

The main store in Berlin at Summit House was a "club worthy of the British troops in Berlin, upon who rest the eyes of American, French, Russians, and other Allied powers stationed in the Metropolis."

Summit House in Berlin

Developers launched a huge scavenging operation to

build the club from the debris of the bombed-out ruins. They took marble from Hermann Goering's Air Ministry and Hitler's Chancellery, the main door came from the Gestapo Headquarters, and ornate marble, imported by the Nazis from Italy, decorated the club's lobby.

The sixties saw the institute pioneer the use of high powered computers, like the Honeywell. It also launched catalogue through Littlewoods and operated a huge distribution depot at Krefeld, along with three bakeries, a 'sports and camping' warehouse and two mineral water factories.

By the mid-seventies, it also offered insurance, loans, hire purchase, as well as rolling out discounts and rewards. Stamp books, ration cards and browsing the monthly 'Naafi News' was part of the fabric of life in the British Armed Forces.

It was undoubtedly the JHQ branch, however, opened in 1972, which was the star attraction. Here, customers could touch and inspect items in clean, hygienic, and bright surroundings. The store boasted a whopping 14,000 square feet of floor space, stuffed with £250,000 worth of stock and was the obvious choice for a demonstration of Naafi competence to Margaret Thatcher when she dropped in for a visit to Rheindahlen in 1977. Here, Mrs. Thatcher was escorted from aisle to aisle, inspecting everything from LP records and shoes to neatly stacked boxes of breakfast cereals.

Naafi remained the target of tabloid hacks, when in 1980 the *Mirror* screamed that Naafi, 'with its cheap drinks' was high on the list of suspects behind the dramatic increase of alcoholic servicemen in Germany. The paper concluded that the BAOR had taken on a new meaning— the 'Boozy Army of the Rhine '—and reported that a top-level inquiry had been ordered into why the squaddies hit the bottle so hard. More than 3,000 servicemen in West Germany were thought to be hooked on booze – and drink-driving arrests leapt from under 400 in 1970 to more than 1,100 in 1979.

"A person could go on the rampage in a tank," stated Brigadier Douglas Wickenden, director of Army psychiatry. The report added that service wives were not much better than their husbands. A military social worker in Hanover said: "Husbands in some garrison areas are said to encourage their wives to anaesthetise themselves with alcohol against loneliness."

When such stories appeared, there was little Naafi could do. Times got tougher for the organisation over coming decades as more service families choose German hypermarkets, or driving over to Holland for the weekly shop.

One successful improvement came in the form of the Britannia Centre which replaced the ageing Summit House as the main Naafi in Berlin in 1990. The Centre was built on the site of Spandau Prison, which was torn-down after the death of its lone inmate Rudolf Hess, Hitler's former deputy. Wittily, customers christened the new Centre "Hessco." Captain Birdseye "personally handed out teddy bears" to 200 "lucky customers" on the opening day (provided their parents had purchased a Birdseye product).

When the Berlin Wall came crashing down in 1989 - the Warsaw Pact was dismantled and the Cold War seemed over. Many still remember when in 1990, the Thatcher government produced *Options for Change*, a review looking to make the most of the 'peace dividend'.

"We are at one of those critical moments in defence policy that occur only once every fifty years," Alan Clark, defence procurement minister, wrote in his diaries at the time. Soon after, the Gulf War created concerns that the cuts were too big and the first time in its history, Naafi recorded losses to the tune of £1.9 million in 1995, with the haemorrhaging topping £4 million the following year.

Not for the first time, the threat of closure loomed, as the implication was, if Naafi could not be saved, it would be ditched.

With that in mind, a huge reorganisation of the entire structure, focused on its traditional core activities; namely, shops and clubs. Naafi drafted in Geoffrey Dart, a skilled retailer from Marks and Spencer to revitalise the business and pare back costs.

He complained forces shops looked ghastly with their poorly lit interiors and linoleum floors, 'they had bad ceilings, bad furniture and poor refrigeration.'

The effects of *Options For Change*, shaped the way British Forces Germany looks today. As for the Naafi, they may only operate in a handful of locations, but it is fitting that it continues to 'serve the services' in Germany.

In making comment about Naafi for my book, former Defence Secretary Michael Heseltine said the institute occupies a unique place in British military history. "Where our armed forces go NAAFI is never far behind. They provide a wonderful service. They build morale. They are there when it matters."

Without a doubt, Naafi will adapt and change in the years to come and I hope it will survive to celebrate its centenary.

Bibliography

Anon, *Naafi Up!*, AQ and DJ Publications, 1996

Cole, Howard, *Naafi in Uniform*, Navy, Army and Air Force Institutes, 1982

Coleman, Lee, *Celebrating 90 Years of Naafi Serving the Services*, Navy Army & Airforce Institutes, 2010

Diett, Eve, *Diary of a Naafi Girl*, Pen Press, 2012

Eden, Anthony, *The Memoirs of Anthony Eden, Earl of Avon, The Reckoning*, Mifflin, 1965

Fortescue, John, *A Short Account of Canteens in the British Army*, Cambridge University Press, 1928

Forty, Anne, *They Also Served, Midas Books*, 1979

Healey, Denis, *Time of My Life*, W W Norton & Co, 1991

Hickman, Tom, *The Call-Up: A History of National Service*, Headline, 2005

Kempe, Frederick, *Berlin 1961*, Berkley, 2012.

Middlebrook, Martin, *The Battle of Hamburg*, Penguin, 1980

Miller, Harry, *Service to the Services*, Newman Neame, 1971

Mitcham, Samuel, *Rommel's Greatest Victory*, Presidio Press, 1998

Murray, John, *I Confess a Memoir of the Siege of Tobruk*, Big Sky, 2011

Phillips, Winifred, *Mum's Army*, Simon & Schuster UK, 2013

Randall, Geoffrey, *The Grocers*, Kogan Page; 2011

Ryle, Sarah, *The Making of Tesco*: A Story of British Shopping, Bantam Press, 2013

Smalley, Edward, *The British Expeditionary Force, 1939-40*, Palgrave Macmillan, 2015

Smith, Kevin, *Letters From the Front: Letters and Diaries from the BEF in Flanders and France*, Fonthill Media, 2013

Thomas, Donald, *An Underworld at War*, John Murray Publishers, 2003

About the Author

Nathan Morley is a journalist based in Nicosia.

As a roving reporter, he has filed for *Deutsche Welle*, ORF and *Vatican Radio* over last two decades, as well as working with *Voice of America* and *Radio Netherlands*.

He enjoyed a decade long career as a news anchor on Cyprus state television and radio, as well as writing extensively for the *Cyprus Mail*.

He is passionate about 20th century European history, and written and broadcast extensively on a variety of subjects; ranging from Erich Honecker, Berlin at war and the Chernobyl disaster, to the history of *Radio Luxembourg*.

Printed in Great Britain
by Amazon

34781793R00173